P9-APR-746

A REVIEW OF PERSONALITY THEORIES

A REVIEW OF PERSONALITY THEORIES

Second Edition

By

VICTOR J. DRAPELA, PH.D.
Professor Emeritus
University of South Florida
Tampa, Florida

CHARLES C THOMAS • PUBLISHER
Springfield • Illinois • U.S.A.

Published and Distributed Throughout the World by

CHARLES C THOMAS • PUBLISHER
2600 South First Street
Springfield, Illinois 62794-9265

ISBN 0-398-95943-8

Library of Congress Catalog Card Number: 94-36205

First Edition, 1987
Second Edition, 1995

With THOMAS BOOKS *careful attention is given to all details of manufacturing and design. It is the Publisher's desire to present books that are satisfactory as to their physical qualities and artistic possibilities and appropriate for their particular use.* THOMAS BOOKS *will be true to those laws of quality that assure a good name and good will.*

Printed in the United States of America
SC-R-3

Library of Congress Cataloging-in-Publication Data

Drapela, Victor J.
A review of personality theories / by Victor J. Drapela.—2nd ed.
p. cm.
Includes bibliographical references and index.
ISBN (invalid) 0-398-95943-8
1. Personality I. Title.
[DNLM: 1. Personality. 2. Psychological Theory. BF 698 D765r 1995]
BF698.D68 1995
155.2—dc20
DNLM/DLC
for Library of Congress 94-36205
CIP

TO MY STUDENTS

PREFACE TO THE FIRST EDITION

WHEN I was in college, one of our professors used to say that our real education would be equal to what we retained after forgetting most of what we had learned from books. This aphorism, contradictory at first sight, has proven its hidden meaning in the process of my professional life. I have certainly forgotten many details about subjects covered in my formal course work. As long as I have retained the core data, however, most related issues have remained clear in my mind. If I need to check on details, I know where to look.

Over the past fifteen years, while teaching Personality Theory courses for hundreds of aspiring counseling practitioners and other helping professionals, I gradually implemented a didactic approach based on the aphorism of my college professor. I focused my efforts on facilitating retention of basic concepts by my students far beyond their graduation date. It is that approach that will explain the origin and rationale of this volume.

My students would use a standard textbook of some 700 pages for detailed study. I did not expect, however, that they would retain the entire content of the textbook beyond the end of the semester (if that far), and certainly not throughout their professional careers. To promote **learning for life** rather than **studying for exams**, I made every effort to help students identify and remember the essentials and form their own skeletal outline of every theory we covered. The long-term outcome of our classroom interaction was the student's ability to use the various personality theories for better understanding of people's internal dynamics and for more successful professional work in the real world.

Most students welcomed my approach and asked me repeatedly for typewritten outlines to help them formulate summaries of the theories we covered. Such requests led to the eventual writing of the present volume. The book may prove useful to students in counselor education and other applied psychology programs, particularly when reviewing personality theories for comprehensive or qualifying examinations. It may also serve as a useful resource to practitioners preparing for certification or licensure tests. Additionally, the information contained in this book may be of interest to persons of many walks of life who want to better understand the many and diverse interpretations of human behavior and of the dynamic forces within personality.

I have made a conscious effort to keep the language clear and simple, avoiding unneeded technical terms. I have, however, given full recognition to the distinctive terminology developed by certain theorists. To lend a degree of concreteness to abstract ideas, explanatory drawings have been included wherever appropriate. This approach will likely benefit visual learners, who seem to be numerous in our days.

V.J.D.

PREFACE TO THE SECOND EDITION

DURING THE seven years since its publication, this book has served as a study guide to many graduate students in counselor education courses. It helped them gain basic insights into various interpretations of the role that personality dynamics assume in human behavior.

The feedback by students who used the book has been very positive. They found the book especially useful for review of the material when preparing for their midterm and final semester examinations. It helped them organize the extensive subject matter into a closely linked, yet clearly differentiated framework. A parallel opinion was also voiced by some former students, working as counselors in the field, who used the book to prepare for the personality and human development sections of the exam required for state licensure.

Some users of the book felt that a more extensive explanation of certain concepts might be helpful, but they also emphasized that, while doing any revisions, I keep intact the two qualities of the book they liked best—its brevity and clarity.

I paid close attention to those comments, and the text of this second edition reflects them. I have followed the original structure of chapters and added new material only where clearly warranted. The basic character of the book has been maintained. I hope, therefore, that this new edition will be even closer attuned to the needs of students whose learning process it is meant to facilitate.

V. J. D.

ACKNOWLEDGMENTS

WHILE PREPARING the manuscript for this book, I received assistance from several persons to whom I am indebted. My wife and professional colleague, Gwen Blavat Drapela, critiqued the entire text and made numerous constructive suggestions for its improvement.

At the University of South Florida I was given assistance during the preparation of both the initial and the revised typescripts: seven years ago, by the staff of the Counselor Education Department; at present, by the staff of the Department of Psychological and Social Foundations, which now incorporates counselor education as one of its academic programs.

My publisher, Charles C Thomas, encouraged me to prepare this second edition of the book and skillfully guided the production process through its stages to the final outcome.

My sincere thanks to all.

CONTENTS

A REVIEW OF PERSONALITY THEORIES

CHAPTER 1

A DYNAMIC VIEW OF PERSONALITY THEORIES

PERSONALITY DYNAMICS

TO UNDERSTAND human behavior, we have to understand the forces that shape it. In every one of us there are many such forces. Some are intrapersonal, related to internal processes within us; others are interpersonal, determining our relationships with people around us. These forces are commonly referred to as **personality dynamics.** The inner world of every person is an intricate structure of such dynamics—physiological, psychological, and social needs that serve as motivational factors. Tensions and conflicts are also present, generated by intrapersonal or environmental pressures.

We understand many of our personality dynamics but not all. Some operate beyond the reach of our awareness; nevertheless, they exert a strong influence on our behavior. Although we perceive our personality to be unified and solid, it is, in fact, in constant flux. It resembles a process rather than a completed structure, a state of ongoing development rather than permanency. Many psychologists view personality as a field or base that contains our current self-perceptions, short- and long-term goals, distinct characteristics, values, and a broad repertoire of life experiences. Continual changes occur within the field as new perceptions enter from outside and earlier incorporated elements are discarded—no longer considered useful or relevant (Combs & Snygg, 1959).

A HISTORICAL PERSPECTIVE

The dynamic nature of personality was not always recognized. Modern psychology, like some other sciences, is the most recent stage of a long developmental process reaching some twenty-five centuries back. In that era and for a long time afterward, psychology was a part of philosophy, "the noble mother of wisdom," in its quest to explore the nature and meaning of the universe, and particularly of the human species. Philosophers such as Aristotle believed that every being was composed of two substantive elements, **matter** and **form.** In humans the material component was the body (soma) and the formal elements the soul (psyche). "Psychologia" was considered the **science of the soul.**

This Aristotelian doctrine was additionally expanded and adjusted to the tenets of Christian theology by a medieval monk and scholar, Thomas Aquinas, who placed major emphasis on the spirituality (and immortality) of the soul. He described personality as an individual substance with a rational nature—a brief and philosophically accurate statement. Unfortunately, it ignored the dynamic nature of personality. It was like a still picture of a person rigidly seated on a chair rather than a videotape of a walker (or runner) that each person is. Later philosophical movements, such as those of Descartes or Kant, although sharply disagreeing with Aquinas, did not provide the dynamic dimension for the concept of personality either. It was the emergence of psychology as an independent science that eventually filled in the missing element and provided a more life-like image of man.

DEFINITIONS OF PERSONALITY

Many definitions of personality have been proposed by psychologists over the past one hundred years. When placed on a continuum, they would fall between two diametrically opposed views: (1) Self-theorists perceive personality as having a real existence and producing real outcomes. (2) Behaviorists, on the other hand, view personality as a mere inference of behavior which is the only directly observable and measurable phenomenon.

The definition proposed here approximates the viewpoint of self-theorists. Personality is defined as a **dynamic source of behavior, identity, and uniqueness** of every person. The term **behavior** covers thought processes, emotions, decision making, bodily activities, social interaction, etc. In a similar vein, Allport (1937) emphasized that "personality **is** something and **does** something" (p. 48). Conversely, Sullivan (1953) viewed personality as a mere pattern of "recurrent interpersonal situations" and Cattell (1950) considered it an aspect of the individual that permits the prediction of behavior. Some authors have been less specific or less willing to offer any substantive definition, leaving it up to the individual observer to decide what definition is most acceptable (Hall & Lindzey, 1978).

THEORIES OF PERSONALITY

Having reviewed some definitions of personality, we shall focus on the nature of theories and see how they can be applied to the study of personality. Generally speaking, a theory is a **framework** that any person can devise on the basis of certain proven facts **for interpreting** some more or less complex issue. Every one of us has been exposed to theories on various issues, from the origin of the universe to effective management styles or the etiology of a particular illness. Some of the theories have been helpful; others did little or nothing to aid us in better understanding the issue involved.

If we apply the concept of theory to the area of personality, it follows that personality theories are frameworks devised by various professionals, mostly psychologists or psychiatrists, to **interpret the interaction of dynamic forces operating in every person's life.** Theorists may focus, for instance, on the primary motivational forces in individuals. To what degree are they physiological, psychological, or social? How does goal orientation develop and how does it impact the individual's life? Theorists explain the development and maturation process of the individual in various ways. Maturity may be interpreted in terms of social adjustment or as personal adequacy devoid of a normative dimension. Some theorists focus on the individual's coping mechanisms in dealing with threat, maintaining a degree of equilibrium, compensating for deficiencies, etc.

Although all theories of personality have originated on the basis of a number of proven data, the data selected by one theorist will significantly differ from data chosen by another. This explains the high degree of variations we find among their theories.

ESSENTIAL QUALITIES OF PERSONALITY THEORIES

To fulfill its basic function, a personality theory has to possess certain qualities. They are not always present to an optimal degree, but without at least a minimal degree of each of them a theory would not be useful. These qualities are as follows:

1. **Clarity of understanding.** If the interpretation of personality dynamics lacks clarity, the understanding of the functioning of personality is not enhanced but clouded. This defies, of course, the main purpose for which a theory is formed.

2. **Logical structure.** Internal contradictions in a theory produce con-

fusion and are potentially damaging to the followers of the theory if they are truly committed to it. In most cases, the followers become aware of the illogical structure and drop the theory. In professional circles, such a theory will quickly fade away.

3. Internal unity. Unless there is a clear linkage among its parts, a theory cannot be persuasive or maintain its integrity. It ceases to be a framework and eventually disintegrates.

4. Uniqueness. To serve a useful purpose, a theory needs to present a new approach to the interpretation of personality dynamics. If that is not the case, the theory is spurious although it may use a new lingo. It is merely a rehash of certain earlier developed theories.

This is not meant to be a negative comment on eclectic theories. Well-designed eclectic theories uniquely combine elements found in other theories and add their own distinct contributions.

RELATIONSHIP OF PERSONALITY THEORIES AND COUNSELING THEORIES

Occasionally, students ask why it is necessary to study theories of personality when they would later take another course on theories of counseling. Valid reasons exist for this seeming duplication: (1) There is a distinction between the two kinds of theories, and professional helpers need to understand that distinction. (2) Counseling theories build on personality theories. Counselors who wish to effectively structure their helping interventions need to have a clear picture of the interplay of personality dynamics in their clients: motivation, responses to threat, coping mechanisms, etc. Without such understanding, they would be working in a vacuum, not knowing which dynamics they are dealing with.

In the counselor-client relationship, **personality theories focus on what goes on in the internal world of clients; counseling theories**, on the other hand, **focus on the attitudes, skills, and techniques counselors should use.** Depending on the view counselors have of the interaction of dynamics within their clients, they will choose their counseling strategies.

Among counseling theorists, there is a significant variety of approaches they recommend. Some originators of counseling schools formulated their own personality theories; others built upon existing theories that originated in the past. Yet, every counseling approach needs to be undergirded by an appropriate theory of personality. In this context, I want to recall a statement by Lewin that there is nothing more practical than a good theory. This admonition has particular significance for counselors and other helping professionals. Without a solid theoretical background, they would lower themselves to the level of mere technicians.

ORGANIZATION OF CHAPTERS

1. A brief biographical sketch of the theorist will precede the exposition of every personality theory. Most theorists projected their experiences and values into their theoretical framework. Thus, understanding their life history will help the reader better grasp the meaning of their propositions and theoretical concepts.
2. The main section of every chapter will be devoted to the explanation of a given theory. As earlier mentioned, whenever appropriate, explanatory drawings will be inserted to accompany the abstract ideas of individual theorists.
3. Every chapter will contain a brief explanation on how each personality theory can be applied to counseling.
4. Review questions, at the end of each chapter, will help the reader recall salient points of the discussed subjects.

HOW TO USE THE BOOK FOR ACADEMIC WORK

In instructional settings, the book will likely be used along with other study aids, such as a full-size textbook or a list of recommended readings. The latter would contain passages selected from **primary sources,** i.e., writings by the originators of various theories explaining their own ideas and concepts. It is particularly helpful to make use of such additional resources for gaining more detailed information on the subject matter, which my book—consistent with its purpose—explains in basic terms.

The sequence of the learning process recommended for the use of this book in academic settings has three stages:

1. Prior to a class lecture, read the chapter explaining the theory that is to be covered by the instructor. If in the process of this reading ambiguities emerge about any of the concepts of the theory, note them for yourself. During the lecture in class, be particularly alert and watch for explanations of those specific concepts. If the ambiguities are not resolved, ask the instructor for clarification of the problem areas. Profes-

sors typically welcome honest questions of this kind; they feel gratified by the students' eagerness to actively participate in the learning process.

2. During every lecture, make copious notes and reread the chapter and your notes shortly afterward to help reconstruct the professor's explanation. If there are still blind spots or if new ambiguities emerge, ask for further clarification at the next class meeting.

3. Try to complement these efforts by the use of resources mentioned earlier—the writings of the theorists themselves. Reaching back in time to the origins of a theory helps the student gain a feeling of "personal contact" with the theorist.

Also, reading pertinent passages in another textbook is a useful approach. It provides additional information and broadens the student's perspective since the theory may be perceived from a somewhat different viewpoint.

CHAPTER REVIEW

1. What is the function of intrapersonal and interpersonal dynamics of personality and to what degree are the dynamics understood by the individual?
2. What is meant by the statement that personality is in constant flux?
3. How was psychology defined by early philosophers in the pre-Christian era and in the Middle Ages?
4. When did the dynamic dimension of personality attain full recognition?
5. What are the two diametrically opposed definitions of personality in contemporary psychology?
6. How can one explain the conflicting personality definitions?
7. What is meant by the concept of theory?
8. How does the concept of theory apply to personality?
9. What are the four essential qualities of personality theories?
10. What is the distinction between personality theories and counseling theories?

REFERENCES

Allport, G. W. (1937). *Personality: A psychological interpretation.* New York: Holt, Rinehart & Winston.

Cattell, R. B. (1950). *Personality: A systematic, theoretical, and factual study.* New York: McGraw Hill.

Combs, A. W., & Snygg, D. (1959). *Individual behavior: A perceptual approach to behavior.* New York: Harper & Row.

Hall, C. S., & Lindzey, G. (1978). *Theories of personality* (3rd ed.). New York: Wiley.

Sullivan, H. S. (1953). *The interpersonal theory of psychiatry.* New York: Norton.

CHAPTER 2

PSYCHOANALYTIC THEORY

SIGMUND FREUD (1856-1939)

IT SEEMS appropriate to begin this review of personality theories with Sigmund Freud, whose psychoanalysis has been an important force of the twentieth century, both in psychology and in the cultural life of most countries of the world.

FREUD'S LIFE

Freud was born in Moravia (eastern part of the Czech Republic) into a large Jewish family. The constellation within the family—a relatively old and stern father and a much younger, loving mother—was threatening to the young Sigmund:

> No wonder he had night terrors, enuresis and hallucinations! No wonder the Oedipus relationships were strikingly delineated or etched in the apperceptions of this strong feeling, determined, brilliant, unusual child. One shudders to think what would have been lost if Sigmund Freud had had normal personality reactions, normal family relationships. (Appel, 1957, pp. 16–17.)

The family moved to Vienna, where Freud spent virtually all his adult life. Yet, he never felt like a true Viennese and never adjusted to the pseudo-Victorian mentality of the Viennese people. His negative view of religion additionally hindered a positive relationship with the Catholic environment of Vienna, in which religion was considered a sign of social propriety and decency. Freud believed that religion originated in the young mankind's fears and in its need for help and he considered religious behavior to be close to neurotic behavior. In a conversation with Binswanger (1957), Freud pointed to his completed manuscript, titled "The future of an illusion," and said with an ironic smile, "I am sorry I cannot satisfy your religious needs" (p. 82).

Although very successful in his medical career, Freud was never truly accepted by his professional peers. Furthermore, he was unable to maintain long-term friendships, even with people who initially revered him as their mentor and intellectual leader. (This was true about Adler, Jung, Rank, and others.) A fairly deep relationship developed for a time between Freud and a Berlin physician, Doctor Wilhelm Fliess, whom Freud called his "alter ego." Schur (1972), who reviewed Freud's correspondence with Fliess, pointed out that for several years the two men had a stimulating exchange of ideas and offered mutual support to each other. Unfortunately, even this relationship waned.

Freud was in ill health through most of his adult life. He had cancer of the jaw that required several surgical interventions. He also suffered from cardiac problems (some believe that he had an undiagnosed heart attack in his early middle age). The fact that he smoked as many as twenty cigars a day did not help either condition. In spite of his torture, however, Freud was able to maintain a calm, devoted relationship with his wife, Martha, and had six children with her.

The subtle intellect of Freud is typified by this brief excerpt from his book on the unconscious manifested in jokes:

> Two Jews met in a railway carriage at a station in Galicia. "Where are you going?" asked one. "To Cracow," was the answer. "What a liar you are!" broke out the other. "If you say you're going to Cracow, you want me to believe you're going to Lemberg. But I know that in fact you're going to Cracow. So why are you lying to me?" (Freud, 1960, p. 115.)

He was able to interpret any contradictory situation in such a way that the outcome would make sense in terms of his designs.

After a long and highly fruitful career, Freud was persuaded by his friends to leave Vienna when Nazi soldiers occupied Austria in 1938. He went to England, where he died one year later.

POINTS OF EMPHASIS IN FREUD'S THEORY

Physiological Determinism

In Freud's view, the individual is pressured by overwhelming **physiological forces** that have a decisive influence on human life. They are major **determinants** of behavior and personality development. To maintain balance in spite of ongoing pressure of instincts and conflicting impulses that operate side-by-side, personality has to be primarily reactive rather than active.

The Sexual Nature of Psychic Energy

Libido is Freud's own term for the psychic energy that animates all functions of personality. Libido is sexual in nature, a point Freud (1949) repeatedly emphasized: "The greater part of what we know about Eros—that is, about its exponent, the libido—has been gained from the study of the sexual functions" (p. 24).

The Unconscious

Freud's view of personality can be likened to an iceberg. The tip that rises above the water level is called the **conscious.** It is that part of personality of which the individual is completely aware. The layer below is called the **preconscious.** It contains ideas, decisions, experiences, or conflicts that were once in a person's awareness but have since been forgotten. They can be recalled without much difficulty. The large layer at the bottom of the imaginary iceberg is the **unconscious.** It is a maze of images, distortions of reality, and desires that lies outside of the individual's awareness. Yet, the unconscious exerts a strong motivating influence on personality functioning and human behavior.

PERSONALITY STRUCTURE

Personality, in Freud's view, is a closed system. Libido, the psychic energy, has to work itself out within the confines of this system—a condition that additionally underscores the earlier-mentioned pressures. Freud postulated three subsystems with mutually conflicting principles and goals that cohabitate within personality and are engaged in an ongoing struggle. They are the id, the ego, and the superego (see Fig. 1).

The Id

Freud (1966) called the id a "dark, inaccessible part of our personality," and "a chaos, a cauldron full of seething excitations" (p. 537). He viewed it as a receptacle and dispenser of libidinal energy. From the depths of the **unconscious,** the id demands instant and complete satisfaction of its cravings. It is **irrational** and operates according to the **pleasure principle.** In its quest for pleasure, the id has no concern for the needs of others.

An infant can be described as an unadulterated id. Occasionally, we may see the id in action when we watch the behavior of a small child held by its mother who tries to buy groceries in a store. The id obtains satisfaction through the **primary process**—a dream-like blending of fantasy and reality that operates at the unconscious level. For instance, an infant who craves for nourishment while no food is forthcoming will fantasize the pleasure of food intake based on such an earlier experience.

Freud (1966) believed that a phenomenon parallel to the primary process can be found in adults—the nocturnal dream. In his view, dreams fulfill the unconscious wishes of adults (Freud, 1955b), as will be further explained in the section on the nature of dreams.

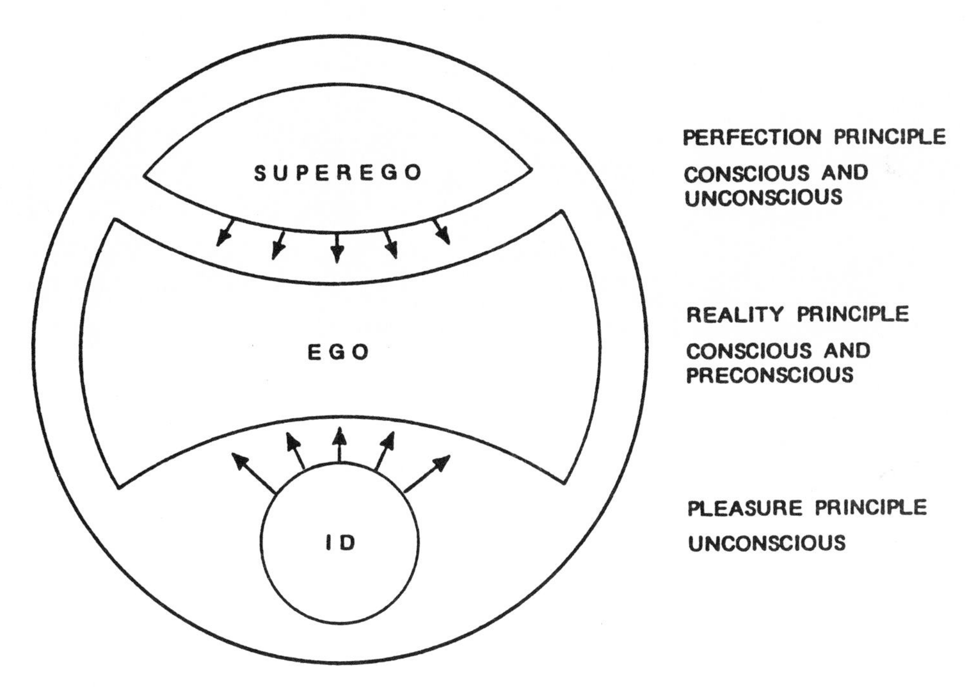

Figure 1. Freud's structure of personality. Arrows emanating from the id are cathexes; arrows emanating from the superego are anticathexes.

The Ego

The ego is guided by the **reality principle.** It translates the demands of the id into practical ways of need-fulfillment by modifying the nature and the timing of the demands. The ego is **rational;** it operates at the **conscious level,** weighing actions and their consequences and storing in the preconscious forgotten events and personal experiences that it may recall.

The operational pattern of the ego is called the **secondary process.** Unlike the primary process based on fantasy and geared to the attainment of pleasure, the secondary process is based on reality and geared to the achievement of genuine need satisfaction. This is done through **reality testing;** desires of the id are tested against the reality in which the individual lives and are adjusted accordingly. A well-developed ego (wide ego span) is the mark of a healthy personality.

The Superego

The superego contains **restrictions** and **prohibitions** imposed upon the infant and small child by parents and significant others. It contains also **praise** given for "good" behavior. The prohibitions of "bad" behavior would, in themselves, not produce the superego, if they were not **interiorized** by the individual. Part of the superego is **conscious,** consisting of the consciously interiorized prohibitions and signs of praise. Many prohibitions and signs of praise, however, were given in infancy, during the weaning or toilet training process, when the individual experienced such signs largely at the unconscious level. They constitute the **unconscious** part of the superego.

Whereas the id demands full and instant pleasure, the superego's reaction can be summarized as follows: No pleasure is to be allowed; instead, perfection is to be attained. The superego can be defined as the moralizing force in personality, based on the **principle of perfection.**

Persons whose superego has not been adequately developed tend to feel little guilt even after major ethical infractions. In extreme cases, their behavior is antisocial or criminal. Conversely, in others the superego has become enormous in its power. These are perfectionists who will eventually suffer from moral anxiety; in extreme cases, they may become dysfunctional.

Interaction of Id, Ego, and Superego

It is important to recognize that Freud perceived personality as a unified entity. The three subsystems are closely interwoven components of personality rather than independent agents. To understand their interaction, we have to identify two concepts: cathexis and anticathexis.

Cathexis can be defined as movement of psychic energy (libido) from the originating subsystem toward a source of gratification. If the source of gratification is external, we speak of **object cathexis,** e.g., the attraction one feels toward a particular activity or the emotional attachment to a person. If the source of gratification is intrapersonal, we speak of **ego cathexis,** i.e., self-love. By generating numerous cathexes of both kinds, the id, from which all psychic energy emanates, fills the entire personality system with surplus energy.

Anticathexis. This is a force that originates in the ego or superego in order to block a cathexis of the id. We seem to face here a logical problem, however, that needs to be resolved. How can we explain the presence of some counteracting energy in the ego and superego, which do not have any direct supply of libido? Blum (1953) explains it by referring to the surplus energy mentioned above, that the id squanders throughout the personality system.

In the process of their formation, the ego and superego trap enough of this surplus energy to make themselves into viable, energized personality subsystems. This indirectly acquired energy explains their subsequent ability to block cathexes emanating from the id. Paradoxically, it is the oversupply of libido provided by the irrational id that makes anticathexes possible.

In infancy, the cathexes of the id are blocked by the interiorized prohibitions of parents (anticathexes of the superego) and eventually by anticathexes of the rational ego. This pattern continues throughout the individual's life, except that in adulthood the role of parents is assumed by other authority figures. Additionally, the superego may at times oppose actions originating in the ego. This happens whenever the ego modifies demands of the id in a less stringent manner than is acceptable to the superego. In most cases, a healthy ego has sufficient strength to resist both the extreme demands of the id and the extreme prohibitions of the superego. The ego assumes the role of a mediator, achieving compromise solutions on the basis of reality testing.

INTRAPERSONAL CONFLICTS

The preceding section has offered clues to conflicts that inevitably arise from such a configuration of personality.

Conflicts of id versus ego occur when the id demands immediate satisfaction and the ego, on the basis of reality testing, is in the process of modifying that demand. For example, a seven-year-old boy wants to steal a toy truck in a department store, but since he has heard about store detectives who detain shoplifters he wonders whether it would not be better to wait until he has enough money to buy the toy truck.

Conflicts of id versus superego involve demands of the id that are challenged by the superego on the basis of their real or alleged unethical nature. We can again use the example of the boy who is tempted to steal a toy truck. This time, however, he hesitates because he is reminded of the commandment that forbids stealing—a recent lesson in his religious education class.

Conflicts of ego versus superego are clashes between the rational ego and the perfection-oriented superego. This occurs when persons wish to engage in behavior they rationally evaluate as ethical but may feel guilty about it because of prohibitions interiorized during their puritanical training.

INSTINCTS

In Freud's (1949) view, "the forces, which we assume to exist behind the tensions caused by the needs of the id are called **instincts.** They represent the somatic demands upon mental life" (p. 19). The term **mental life** should be understood as the psychological domain of the individual. Freud's view of instincts involves the following points: (1) instincts are inborn; (2) they are attached to the id; and (3) they serve as psychological expressions of somatic tension.

Although Freud recognized the existence of numerous instincts, he singled out only two instincts as basic, **Eros** and **Thanatos.** By their nature, Eros and Thanatos move in different directions, but occasionally they link with each other. Both instincts are present in every person but not to the same degree. One of them always predominates.

Eros, the Life Instinct

Eros is guided by the **pleasure principle.** Its main drive is sexual, leading to intimate union and eventually to procreation of new life. Eros is related to various parts of the body called **erogenous zones,** which are sensitive to stimulation that induces pleasure. These zones play a major role in the functioning of the life instinct; they are also closely related to the stages of personality development that will be discussed later.

Thanatos, the Death Instinct

Thanatos is characterized by destructiveness and follows the **nirvana principle.** Nirvana symbolizes the absence of suffering and total peace that every person will eventually find in death. Prior to death, however, there is the process of destruction or slow disintegration. Thanatos is manifested by rage and aggressive behavior that may be directed toward others or self. Freud even considers the possibility of Eros turning into Thanatos, when sexual love changes into sexual aggressiveness and the lover becomes a sex murderer.

DEVELOPMENT OF PERSONALITY

Freud structured the development of personality in terms of five dynamic stages. The initial stages are in direct relationship with the earlier-mentioned **erogenous zones** of the human body. Although he believed that, strictly speaking, the individual's entire physique is responsive to pleasure, Freud singled out three areas as particularly pleasure-prone.

These erogenous zones include: (1) **the oral zone** that contains the lips and the inside of the mouth; (2) **the anal zone** that contains the rectal area; and (3) **the phallic zone** that contains the sexual organs.

In earlier days, Freud's developmental stages have been usually identified in terms of the child's age; e.g., from birth to age two was assumed to be the oral stage, etc. This chronological approach is, however, confusing in the context of the 1990s, when the maturation process in childhood is faster than in past generations. This explains why I have omitted identifying developmental stages by the child's age.

The Oral Stage

The newly born child derives its pleasure from receiving nourishment. Initially, this involves **sucking** and **swallowing.** These pleasurable experiences, however, become less satisfying as the child is weaned and during the teething period when the oral cavity, earlier the center of pleasure, becomes the source of pain.

The Anal Stage

The child shifts its attention to the anal region, where it experiences the pleasure of relieving pressure in its lower intestine through **spontaneous bowel movements.** For a time, these pleasurable experiences are tolerated by the parents. But eventually even this source of satisfaction is removed in the process of toilet training. The child has to assume control over its bowel movements and endure anal pressure.

The Phallic Stage

At this stage the child focuses its attention on the genital region, explores its own genitals, and engages in sexual fantasies. Autoerotic behavior emerges; the child is allured by the pleasure brought about through masturbation. During this stage the **Oedipus conflict** (in boys) or the **Electra conflict** (in girls) occurs. The child falls in love with the parent of the opposite sex and feels hostility toward the parent of the same sex. The boy who maintains erotic feelings toward his mother fears that his father will castrate him (**castration anxiety**); the girl who is erotically attracted to her father is frustrated since she lacks a part of her father's anatomy)—the penis (**penis envy**).

These conflicts are eventually resolved through the process of identification with the parent of the same sex, which leads to repression of incestuous desires for the parent of the opposite sex. The boy wants to be like his father, the girl wants to resemble her mother. Freud believed, however, that the identification process of girls occurred later in life and that the Electra conflict was never fully resolved.

Latency Period

This stage is characterized by an apparent dormancy of sexual impulses. Libido is channeled into school work, group activities, and newly discovered recreational pursuits. Freud (1966) called the latency period "a halt and retrogression in sexual development," a time in which earlier impulses and experiences "fall victim to infantile amnesia—the forgetting, which veils our earliest youth from us and makes us strangers to it" (p. 326). It is that forgotten psychic material that psychoanalytic treatment intends to bring back to one's consciousness.

Genital Stage

This stage begins at puberty, at which time the libido erupts with new vigor. The autoerotic patterns of the pre-latency years are gone; the individual is heterosexually oriented and moves toward genuine erotic relationships and genital behavior. This is the final developmental stage that serves as entry to adulthood.

DEFENSE MECHANISMS

To protect itself against threatening thoughts or desires that may lead to anxiety, the ego may take drastic actions to eliminate such danger. These actions are called defense mechanisms, and they operate at the **unconscious** level. A major contribution to the understanding of individual defense mechanisms was made by Anna Freud (1937). In this section, we shall cover four defense mechanisms that are fairly common—repression, sublimation, regression, and fixation.

Repression

Repression is an **irrational flight** from unacceptable thoughts and desires, mostly of a sexual nature. The ego, rather than using the secondary process, i.e., reality testing, prior to making a decision, pushes the threatening thought or desire irrationally into the unconscious. That does not, of course, eliminate the libido, which has been the driving force behind the repressed material. In fact, the threat becomes more pronounced, additional defenses have to be built, and eventually a debilitating tug-of-war situation develops between the id and the ego that leads to anxiety.

Repression is often hard to identify because the symptoms it generates are not clearly linked with the real problem. When we squeeze a balloon on one side we create a bulge on the other. The side that has been squeezed may not show, the bulge does. A person who represses a threatening sexual desire may show irritability, lack of concentration, or lack of concern for others. The cause of these symptoms, however, is hidden from the view of most observers.

There is only one effective alternative to repression: dealing with the threatening material at the conscious level, using rational judgment, and making a balanced decision.

Sublimation

Sublimation is a process of **rechanneling** libido from sexual gratification to an activity that society considers admirable, particularly in science and the arts. This process is usually very effective because it avoids a direct clash with the libido and uses sexual energy for creative purposes. For example, a renaissance artist-monk, who is tempted to be intimate with a woman he secretly loves, goes instead to his studio and creates a painting of a biblical scene.

Regression and Fixation

When threats inherent in the genital stage (adult life) become too severe, the ego has a tendency to temporarily regress to a lower stage that has proven to be less stressful. We speak of regression to the oral stage if someone has a tendency to eat or drink excessively whenever exposed to severe pressure. Regression to the anal stage would mean that the person under stress would tend to neglect hygienic needs or orderliness in his or her daily life.

Whereas regression is temporary, fixation is relatively long-lasting. Individuals typically regress to and are fixated at the same developmental stage.

ANXIETY AND FEAR

Freud (1955a) made a clear distinction between anxiety and fear: "Anxiety describes a particular state of expecting the danger or preparing for it, even though it may be an unknown one. Fear requires a definite object of which to be afraid" (p. 12). Both anxiety and fear are emotional responses to threat. Fear focuses on a real and well-differentiated threat, whereas anxiety is responding to an undifferentiated or imaginary threat.

Two types of anxiety will be briefly explained. They are **neurotic anxiety** and **moral anxiety.** Persons suffering from anxiety fear that they will be unable to control their instincts and that they will engage in unacceptable behavior. In neurotic anxiety, they fear forthcoming punishment from society or from an outside authority figure. In moral anxiety, they are afraid of the feelings of guilt that will be imposed upon them by the superego. No matter which anxiety a person may suffer from, it is a painful and debilitating condition.

THE NATURE OF DREAMS

Freud (1966) called dreams "guardians of sleep which get rid of disturbances of sleep" (p. 129). In his view, dreams were able to dispose of stimuli that would otherwise interrupt the individual's sleep. Freud (1955b) asserted that dreams provided a clear insight into a person's **unconscious wishes,** and he offered numerous examples to bolster his claim that dreams are, in fact, the **fulfillment** of unconscious wishes.

In every dream we can recognize the residue of the day (material related to the day's experiences) that merges with the unconscious. There is a **manifest** and a **latent meaning** in dreams—the former understood by the individual who had the dream, the latter a challenge for the interpreting therapist.

Freud (1966) offers an example that clarifies (1) the dream's capacity to fulfill unconscious wishes and (2) the difference between manifest and latent meanings of a dream. He comments on a person's dream about his brother: "[The statement] 'I saw my brother in a box (Kasten)' is not to be translated 'my brother is restricting himself (schränkt sich ein)' but 'I should like my brother to restrict himself: *my brother must restrict himself*' " (Freud 1966, p. 129).

In Freud's view, this dream fulfilled the unconscious wish of the person who wanted to see a major change in his brother's behavior—a willingness to restrict himself. The fulfillment of the unconscious wish was contained in the manifest meaning of the dream—the brother was restricted in a box. Yet, the dream wouldn't make any sense without one's awareness of the latent meaning of the dream—the unconscious wish that stimulated it.

Parenthetically, a brief note should be made of another way in which the unconscious manifests itself in adult life. Freud called these manifestations **parapraxes.** These are overt actions with unconscious connotations, e.g., forgetting to bring certain documents to a meeting or losing one's wedding ring. The verbal variety of parapraxes is the well-known Freudian slip.

APPLICATIONS TO COUNSELING

Freud's theory of personality finds direct application in the practice of classical psychoanalysis and modified psychoanalytic therapy. Yet even counselors who do not accept the psychoanalytic approach as their counseling orientation may better understand the intrapersonal dynamics of their clients by applying elements of Freud's personality theory. These elements may include:

1. Freud's dynamic structure of personality
2. The defense mechanisms
3. Influences of childhood experiences on adult behavior
4. Unconscious and sexual motivation
5. Nature of intrapersonal conflicts

CHAPTER REVIEW

1. What do you know about Freud's life, and what has impressed you most in his biography?
2. What are the main points emphasized in psychoanalytic theory?
3. What is meant by personality being a closed system?
4. Can you explain the nature and functions of the id, the ego, and the superego?
5. What is meant by cathexis and anticathexis?
6. Which three types of intrapersonal conflicts does Freud's theory suggest?
7. What is meant by Eros and Thanatos?
8. Can you explain the Freudian stages of personality development?
9. What is the nature of defense mechanisms and which defense mechanisms can you define?
10. What is the difference between fear and anxiety, and which types of anxiety can you identify?
11. What is the nature of dreams and what are parapraxes?
12. Which elements of Freud's theory may be useful to counselors for interpreting intrapersonal dynamics in clients?

REFERENCES

Appel, K. E. (1957). Freud and psychiatry. In I. Galdston (Ed.). *Freud and contemporary culture* (pp. 3–28). New York: International Universities Press.

Binswanger, L. (1957). *Sigmund Freud: Reminiscences of a friendship.* New York: Grune & Stratton.

Blum, G. S. (1953). *Psychoanalytic theories of personality.* New York: McGraw-Hill.

Freud, A. (1937). *The ego and the mechanisms of defense.* London: Hogarth Press.

Freud, S. (1949). *An outline of psychoanalysis.* New York: Norton.

Freud, S. (1955a). Beyond the pleasure principle. In *Standard edition* (Vol. 18). London: Hogarth Press.

Freud, S. (1966). *The complete introductory lectures on psychoanalysis.* New York: Norton.

Freud, S. (1955b). The interpretation of dreams: First part. In *Standard edition* (Vol. 4). London: Hogarth Press.

Freud, S. (1960). *Jokes and their relation to the unconscious.* New York: Norton.

Schur, M. (1972). *Freud: Living and dying.* New York: International Universities Press.

CHAPTER 3

ANALYTIC THEORY

CARL GUSTAV JUNG (1875-1961)

CARL GUSTAV JUNG is the founder of the analytic school of psychology, which in his lifetime strongly influenced not only psychological science but also the realms of literature and art. Although very broad and balanced in its perspective on human life, Jung's theory has become less influential in later years.

Many psychologists of the past two generations perceived Jung's ideas as overly abstract. The structure of Jung's theory appeared quite complex and it seemed to lack a strong unifying principle, such as the sexual dimension that permeates psychoanalysis or the social emphasis in Adler's theory. Nevertheless, even today Jung has his dedicated followers who compensate for their relatively small number by strong personal commitment.

JUNG'S LIFE

Jung was Swiss and throughout his life he exemplified some of the predominant characteristics of his nation: rugged individualism, thoroughness, and commitment to the work ethic. His father's professional standing as a minister placed him in a respected social stratum. In contrast to Freud, he experienced the gratification of professional acceptance, respect by the general population, and financial independence. Although he befriended Freud and maintained close contact with him for several years, he did not hesitate to break off the relationship when their views clashed and Freud tended to overemphasize his personal authority.

Jung's penchant for a self-selected, often unconventional, life-style is evident from the following description of the home he built for himself:

> Long after his troubles with Freud were over Jung set out to build a house of his own beside the beautiful upper lake of Zurich "because," he said, "I wanted

to make a confession of faith in stone." In 1923, the first round house at Bollingen was built, and at intervals of four years he added fresh structures until finally, in 1931, with dark symbolic intent he extended the tower-like annex because, "I wanted a room in this tower where I could exist for myself alone."

> Calling upon Jung at Bollingen, one first confronted and knocked on a heavy wooden door set in a thick stone wall which in turn seemed to have grown out of the earth. The wall, the door and the oddly shaped towers rising beyond it all, seemed medieval. It was not uncommon, as you waited outside, to hear the ringing sound of an axe falling upon wood because there was no coal, gas or electricity in this strange house and Jung lit his own oil lamps and chopped his own wood. (Brome, 1967, pp. 226–227.)

Although heavily involved in academic work and research as university professor and clinician, he found sufficient time to work through a period of self-imposed "creative illness"—daily analyzing his dreams and recording his insights. Eventually, he became convinced that his work was as much art as it was science. He also traveled extensively, often to other continents, to observe unique cultures, e.g., those of Indian tribes in America and of natives in Africa, India, and Ceylon.

Jung's scientific and cultural interests were very broad. In addition to psychology, he was also well versed in philosophy, anthropology, history, religion, mythology, and medieval astrology. The wide scope of his erudition proved, however, to be a mixed blessing. When explaining some psychological concept of his theory, Jung links the explanation to various historical and religious observations. He often intensifies the aura of mystery that penetrates all his writings without providing a more comprehensive understanding of his concepts. Among personality theories, his is one of the more difficult to grasp.

POINTS OF EMPHASIS IN JUNG'S THEORY

Personality—An Autonomous System

Although accepting many tenets of psychoanalysis, Jung did not consider sexual instincts the major determinants of human behavior. He structured personality, which he called **psyche**, as an autonomous system. Every person was to be able to express his or her individuality and uniqueness in relationship with the environment. The ego was meant to be active rather than reactive.

Expanded View of the Past

Jung placed emphasis on the individual's past. However, unlike psychoanalysis, which showed interest in past experiences only from the person's physical birth on (**ontogenetic** dimension), Jung extended his perspective of the past far beyond that point. He also included animal ancestry and prehistoric and historic human ancestry (**phylogenetic** dimension).

A New Perspective of the Unconscious

Jung perceived the unconscious in more positive terms than did classical psychoanalysis. Also, his view was broader, postulating (1) an inherited **collective unconscious** and (2) an acquired **personal unconscious** —concepts that will be explained later in this chapter.

Self-Realization and Wholeness

Jung considered a mature, well-adjusted person one who has achieved a high degree of **self-realization.** This principle places Jung in company with phenomenologists and self-theorists. He formulated parallel ideas far ahead of their general acceptance in professional circles and by the public. Another closely related concept in personal adjustment, coined by Jung, was **wholeness**—a thorough integration of personality.

STRUCTURE OF THE PSYCHE

In Jung's view, personality, the psyche, consists of four major subsystems: (1) the collective unconscious; (2) the personal unconscious; (3) the ego, which is the center of consciousness; and (4) the self, which links the conscious with the unconscious (see Fig. 2).

Jung (1966a) called psychic energy "libido" but emphasized that the term was used in a much broader sense than in psychoanalysis, without sexual connotations: "Libido for me means psychic energy, which is equivalent to the intensity with which psychic contents are charged. Freud, in accordance with his theoretical assumptions, identifies Libido with Eros and tries to distinguish it from psychic energy in general" (pp. 52–53).

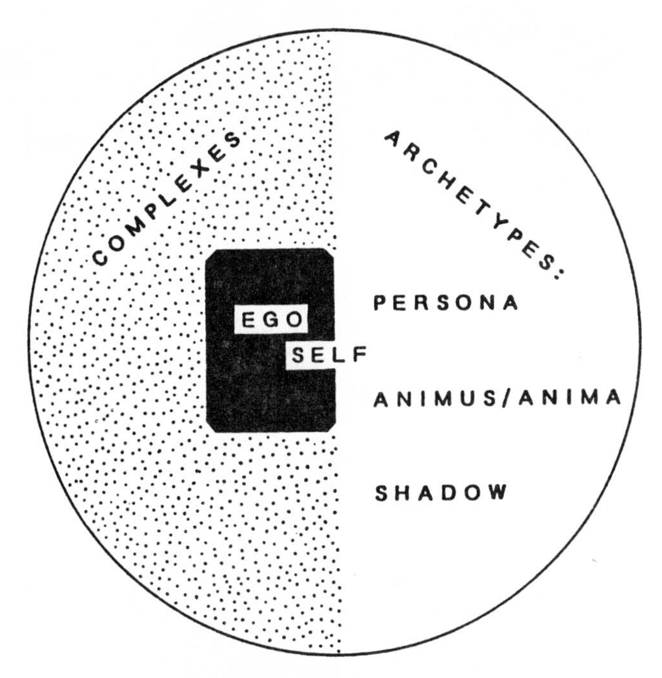

Figure 2. Jung's structure of personality (psyche).

The Collective Unconscious

The psyche has **inherited** this part of the unconscious: it is linked to the past and "comprises in itself the psychic life of our ancestors right back to the earliest beginnings" (Jung, 1969b, p. 112). The collective unconscious is the deepest common denominator of all humans, by which a person's "mind widens out and merges into the mind of mankind, . . . where we are all the same" (Jung, 1968, p. 46). The collective unconscious contains experiences of both human and animal ancestors, some of them disturbing, others satisfying. In contrast with Freud's theory, which perceives the unconscious as a potential threat to the person's conscious ego, Jung presents his collective unconscious as a potential source of wisdom in human life.

To explain Jung's theory of ancestral influences on the psyche, Jacobi (1962) proposed the structure of a psychic family tree: "At the very bottom lies the unfathomable, the 'central energy,' out of which the individual psyche has been differentiated" (p. 34). This central energy flows to the psyche through a series of ancestral layers (see Fig. 3). The layers include animal ancestry and prehistoric as well as historic human ancestry—the individual's ethnic group, nation, tribe, and family. As a great river deposits sediments from many regions in its delta, so does the central energy transmit experiences of many ancestral generations to the psyche. The culmination of this process is the emergence of an individual person.

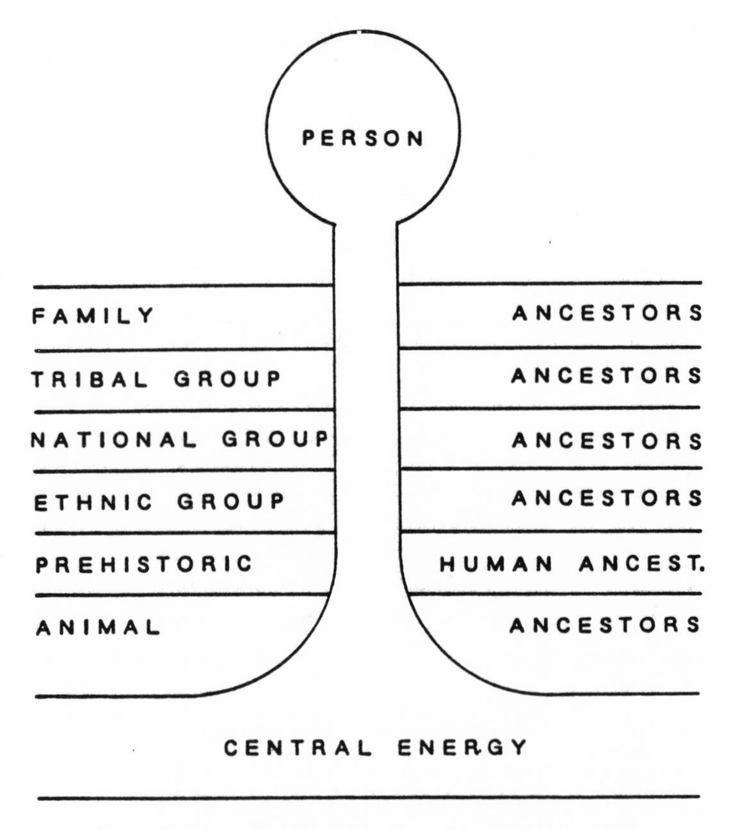

Figure 3. Flow of central energy to the psyche (person).

Archetypes

The collective unconscious harbors numerous ancestral mysteries, kernels of primordial images tied to natural phenomena, and tendencies charged with strong emotional content. Jung called them "archetypes," a term he adopted from the writing of an early Christian scholar, Augustine. He likened them to the axial system of crystals, each having the real crystal preformed within itself. In a similar way, every archetype contains a nucleus of an image, meaning, or distinct pattern of behavior (Jacobi, 1962). Archetypes facilitate the formation of concrete images, which lead to the recognition of real life events or persons prefigured by the archetypes.

The following images can serve as examples of archetypes: birth and death, god, the hero, the old wise man, the great mother, and the child. The German author, Hermann Hesse (1965), who for a time was in therapy with a follower of Jung, offered his own perception of the great mother archetype: "The beautiful woman smiled with dignity. Her gaze was fulfillment, her greeting a homecoming. Silently I stretched my hands out to her. She took both of them in her firm, warm hands. 'You are Sinclair. I recognized you at once. Welcome!' Her voice was deep and warm. I drank it up like sweet wine" (p. 144).

Certain archetypes have been differentiated as independent entities. They are: the persona, the animus and the anima, the shadow, and the self. (Because of a wider role it plays in the psyche, the self will be discussed separately.)

The persona is an archetype that helps the individual maintain his or her individuality while fulfilling certain expectations of society with respect to its mores, values, and conventional behavior in general. Jung (1966b) calls it "a kind of mask, designed on the one hand to make a definite impression upon others, and, on the other, to conceal the true nature of the individual" (p. 192). The persona is a very useful mechanism, as long as it does not become predominant in the psyche, replacing the individual's conscious decisions by conformist attitudes. The archetypal nature of the persona is related only to the **principle** of combining social acceptance with personal independence. The actual behaviors expected or tolerated by society change, of course, from one generation to another.

The animus and the anima are two modalities of the same archetype, one present in women, the other in men. The animus helps women understand and appreciate the maleness of men. It also brings about a degree of male characteristics in women's behavior. Jung (1966b) believed that while the archetype is beneficial in itself, it could become detrimental if used improperly: "A woman possessed by the animus is always in danger of losing her femininity, her adapted feminine persona . . . These psychic changes of sex are due entirely to the fact that a function which belongs inside has been turned outside" (p. 209).

What the animus is to women, the anima is to men, offering them the same benefits and harboring the same dangers for them as it does in the opposite sex. It should be added that Jung's theory, by introducing the animus/anima archetype, offers a basis for a psychological interpretation of bisexuality in humans.

The shadow is an archetype that represents the animal side in every individual, the tendency toward primitive forms of life typical of our animal ancestors. Jung (1966a) believed that every human being is wearing a veneer of civilization over a brute that hides within. Yet, the shadow should be accepted as an integral part of personality and treated as "one's other side." As the visible shadow in bright sunlight emphasizes the realness and plasticity of a human being, so does the archetypal shadow add realness and plasticity to the psyche. The shadow may be seen as Jung's closest parallel to Freud's instinctual side of personality.

The Personal Unconscious

The personal unconscious has been **acquired** by the individual rather than inherited from the past. It emerged from feelings, thoughts, and interpersonal experiences that have been forgotten, repressed, suppressed, or that have otherwise lapsed from consciousness. Jung's (1966b) own remarks make the personal unconscious very similar to the preconscious of Freud: "The materials contained in this layer are of a personal nature in so far as they have the character partly of acquisitions derived from the individual's life and partly of psychological factors which could just as well be conscious" (pp. 135–136).

Complexes

The personal unconscious stores many such materials tied to a person's experiences in life. Jung (1933) called them **complexes**—a term that originated with him—and considered them psychic entities which have escaped the control of a person's consciousness. They have their own existence in the "dark sphere" of the psyche.

Complexes usually evolve from constellations of experiences—thoughts, decisions, and actions. One experience will attract other experiences, that appear similar in nature, and the emotional power of the complex is increased. In general terms, the strength of a complex depends (1) on the impact of the experience in relation to the environment and (2) on the individual's affective disposition and character (Jung, 1969b).

Complexes emerge from significant, often traumatic, personal experiences. They represent a person's "unfinished issues" in life, frequently linked to relationships with "significant others," e.g., parental or other authority figures. Unresolved complexes are potentially quite harmful to personal development. However, as a result of conscious efforts, a complex can be resolved and produce beneficial outcomes in life, such as insights.

The Ego and the Self

Jung believed that the ego and the self should closely interact with each other for the individual's benefit. As the conscious mind, the ego is responsible for the person's ongoing identity and behavior—reasoning, feeling, decision making, and goal-oriented striving. Jung (1969b) compared the ego with an army commander who is called upon to be in charge. Yet, the ego, by itself, is not capable of offering the heights of developmental opportunities that are available to the individual.

In Jung's view it is the self that serves as the most powerful catalyst of internal growth of a person. The self fosters a balanced synthesis of conscious and unconscious processes and facilitates the linkage of the psyche with external forces of growth—the divine and nature: "It is a symbol which unites the opposites; a mediator, bringer of healing, that is, one who makes whole" (Jung, 1969a, p. 164).

Because of these characteristics, the self can significantly enrich the conscious ego and promote self-realization and wholeness of the individual. Jung (1966b) eventually concluded that the self is "supraordinate to the conscious ego. It embraces not only the conscious but also the unconscious psyche, and is therefore, so to speak, a personality which we **also** are" (p. 177). Jung considered the self the "primal, unfathomable ground of the psyche" (Jacobi, 1962) and the central point of personality that maintains equilibrium in life.

DEVELOPMENT OF PERSONALITY

Throughout life, the individual has to be aware of his or her "**personal vocation,**" which Jung (1964) defined as "an irrational factor that destines a man to emancipate himself from the herd and from its well-worn paths" (p. 175). The personal vocation is a great challenge but is not the prerogative of a chosen few. Everyone is unique by nature and has the opportunity to avoid living the life of a mass-produced "normal person" molded by unimaginative educational processes.

Unlike Freud, Jung did not offer clearly defined stages of psychological development in human life. The one major developmental turn in a person's life occurs in the late thirties or early forties, and it is linked with the ego-self relationship. Whereas in the first half of life a person tends to give preeminence to the conscious ego, in the second half of life more emphasis is placed on the synthesis of conscious and unconscious processes offered by the self. Jung (1966b) considered this shift a "new equilibrium, a new centering of the total personality" (p. 221). In concrete terms, it means that in mid-life the person's interests tend to change from primarily physical and material concerns to philosophical, cultural, or religious involvements.

Jung recognized certain obstacles to growth and episodes of maladaptive development that impede true self-realization. Whenever the self is hindered by the ego in its quest for balance of energy in the psyche, some powerful complex might affect the ego and usurp domination of the personality, "the result being a momentary and unconscious alteration of personality known as identification with the complex. In the Middle Ages it went by another name: it was called **possession**" (Jung, 1969b, p. 98). Such identification with a complex leads to a neurotic dissociation of personality, e.g., to the development of multiple personalities.

JUNG'S TYPOLOGY

Although many of Jung's ideas have not survived in the competition with newer personality theories, his typology is still used. Jung (1971) distinguished between the attitudes of **introversion** and **extraversion** – focusing on the intrapsychic world or on the environment of the individual. Although both attitudes are present in every person, one is more influential than the other.

Additionally, the personality type is differentiated according to the relative strength of four "faculties" or **psychological functions.** Jung (1969b) explains their nature according to specific contributions that each of them makes:

Thinking inquires about what a perceived object is.
Feeling assesses the value of an object.
Sensation covers sense perception in general.
Intuition establishes the hidden meaning of an object.

The combination and interaction of the two attitudes and the four faculties has produced a broad taxonomy of human types.

DISPLACEMENT OF PSYCHIC ENERGY

Psychic energy can be transferred from one subsystem to another and channeled from one activity to another. Jung (1966a,b; 1969b) dealt with displacement in terms of repression, sublimation, and symbolization.

Unlike **repression** in Freud's theory, the Jungian concept is broader, not exclusively focusing on instinctually stimulated desires or thoughts. One can repress thoughts and desires that have any content. Jung did not see repression as a healthy way of displacing energy; the repressed material generates undue pressure in the unconscious. Since the flow of energy from one subsystem to the other is unhindered, surplus energy from the unconscious will likely flow into the ego and affect conscious processes.

Jung's **sublimation** has similar merits as the parallel concept of Freud since the displaced energy is used for worthwhile purposes. Instead of overloading a subsystem of the psyche by pushing energy in the unconscious, sublimation channels energy from a less socialized behavior to a socially acceptable or culturally higher process.

Symbolization is another useful means of displacing energy to more acceptable pursuits. Instinctual impulses are, for instance, channeled into ritual tribal dances or even into religious ceremonies, which use numerous symbols. By this process the energy-laden instinct obtains vicarious satisfaction and its force is deflated. Civilization itself is the outcome of numerous symbolizations.

APPLICATIONS TO COUNSELING

In its entirety Jung's theory of personality may find few adherents among current counseling practitioners in this country. Jung's writings are, however, among the classics of psychological literature, and professional counselors may wish to be acquainted with their basic content. Jung has effectively modified classical psychoanalytic views on the unconscious, on the strength of instinctual pressures, and on the nature of intrapersonal dynamics.

Some points of Jung's theory that may find direct application in counseling practice are:

1. His emphasis on self-realization and personal uniqueness
2. His concept of inherited archetypes, especially the unifying self
3. His view of complexes in the personality
4. The basic segments of his typology (the Myers-Briggs Type Indicator test is used by numerous counseling practitioners)

CHAPTER REVIEW

1. How do you view Jung's life history, especially in comparison with Freud's biography?
2. What are the main points of Jung's personality theory?
3. What components are involved in the structure of the psyche?
4. What is meant by the collective unconscious?
5. What is the definition of an archetype?
6. Which archetypes have developed into independent entities?
7. How would you explain the personal unconscious and the complexes?
8. How does Jung envision the interaction of the ego and the self?
9. What is Jung's view of a major developmental turn toward full maturity and self-realization?
10. What is involved in the typology of Jung?
11. Which kinds of displacement of psychic energy does Jung discuss?
12. Which of Jung's concepts can today's counselors incorporate in their practice?

REFERENCES

Brome, V. (1967). *Freud and his early circle: The struggle of psycho-analysis.* London: Heinemann.

Hesse, H. (1965). *Demian: Emil Sinclair's youth.* New York: Harper & Row.
Jacobi, J. (1962). *The psychology of C. G. Jung: An introduction with illustrations.* New Haven: Yale University Press.
Jung, C. G. (1968). *Analytical psychology: Its theory and practice.* London: Routledge & Kegan Paul.
Jung, C. G. (1969a). The archetypes and the collective unconscious. In *Collected works* (Vol. 9, Part 1). Princeton, NJ: Princeton University Press.
Jung, C. G. (1964). *The development of personality.* New York: Pantheon.
Jung, C. G. (1933). *Modern man in search of a soul.* New York: Harcourt, Brace & World.
Jung, C. G. (1966a). On the psychology of the unconscious. In *Collected works* (Vol. 7). New York: Pantheon.
Jung, C. G. (1971). Psychological types. In *Collected works* (Vol. 6). Princeton, NJ: Princeton University Press.
Jung, C. G. (1966b). The relations between the ego and the unconscious. In *Collected works* (Vol. 7). New York: Pantheon.
Jung, C. G. (1969b). The structure and dynamics of the psyche. In *Collected works* (Vol. 8). Princeton, NJ: Princeton University Press.

CHAPTER 4

INDIVIDUAL PSYCHOLOGY

ALFRED ADLER (1870–1937)

ADLER was the founder of a psychological theory which significantly deviated from psychoanalysis by its emphasis on a person's social involvement. It became known as individual psychology, or the second school of Viennese psychology (Freud's being the first). Adler's concept of personality as a unified, purposeful system has exerted a major influence on several generations of psychologists and educators. In this country, Adler's ideas have been promoted by the North American Society of Adlerian Psychology, with offices in New York and Los Angeles and with headquarters in Chicago.

ADLER'S LIFE

Although Jewish by birth, Adler did not suffer from the cultural alienation experienced by Freud in the Catholic environment of Vienna. His biographer, Phyllis Bottome (1939), emphasized that "Adler was a Viennese to the last drop of his blood" (p. 43). He did not overly emphasize his Jewish background; in fact, in his mid-thirties he joined the Protestant faith, since he considered it culturally broader than Judaism.

As a child, Adler suffered from rickets and felt quite disadvantaged, as he sat around in bandages while his peers were having fun. But in spite of that, he had a socially satisfying childhood. Neighborhood children of varied cultural backgrounds made him feel at home in their midst. He was not overly interested in school work, and for a time, his academic future was in doubt. Eventually, however, he changed his ways, entered the University of Vienna, and earned a doctorate in medicine. Before choosing psychiatry as his life's vocation, he worked as general practitioner and ophthalmologist.

For several years Adler had a cooperative relationship with Freud and even served as president of the Psychoanalytic Society. Yet, he never considered himself to be Freud's "disciple" and was never psychoanalyzed. His association with Freud's circle came to an end when members of the Psychoanalytic Society opposed Adler's views and ratified their opposition by a formal vote. He then founded his own professional society.

From early youth, Adler was concerned about social injustice and poverty. While studying social issues, he became interested in the writings of Karl Marx and in the socialist movement in general. He made no secret of his conviction that "only in socialism would social interest (Gemeinsinn), as the demand for unhindered living together, remain the final goal and purpose" (Adler, 1964, p. 313).

Only much later did he become disenchanted by the harsh practices of Marxist officialdom in the Soviet Union. He rejected these excesses—"the intoxication of power has seduced them" (Adler, 1964, p. 315)—but he never lost his admiration for socialist ideals. This ideological bent had another important effect on his life. It was at a socialist political gathering that he met Raissa Epstein, a Russian by birth and a revolutionary by conviction. At first, the two believed that ideologically they had much in common. After they got married, however, it became evident that Adler's brand of socialism was much too tame in contrast to the radicalism of his wife.

Another problem area emerged when Raissa objected to the male dominance typical of the Austrian middle-class family of the period. Adler's behavior, moreover, was not always predictable: "He could be endearing, affectionate, arrogant, infuriating by turns and was certainly a man of moods" (Brome, 1967, p. 17). In these circumstances, Raissa suffered from feelings of dejection and for a short period of time left her husband who was totally absorbed by his career. She knew by then that she could not participate in the professional work of her husband to the extent that she had hoped. Bottome (1939) believed that in the final analysis, it was Adler's involvement in psychology that placed a barrier between him and his wife. Yet, in spite of these problems, the couple developed a harmonious relationship and raised three children.

In the 1920s, Adler organized, with the support of the Vienna Educational Board, a number of child guidance centers, which he staffed with his adherents. For over ten years these centers functioned quite successfully until the new political climate of the 1930s forced their closure. Adler was a prolific lecturer and was frequently invited to speak in the United States. Eventually, he moved to this country and promoted his movement among psychiatrists, counselors, and educators. He died in 1937 during a lecture tour in the United Kingdom.

POINTS OF EMPHASIS IN ADLER'S THEORY

Striving for Superiority

In Adler's view, every person is striving to overcome **feelings of inferiority** inherent in childhood and to attain superiority. This basic assumption of Adler is in sharp contrast to the significance of instinctual drives and the pleasure principle of Freud.

Social Emphasis

Only when the striving for **superiority** is **socially oriented** does it enhance the individual. Self-centered, **antisocial striving** for superiority is regressive; Adler considered it the source of behavioral deviations and failures of character. Healthy expressions of superiority are characterized by endeavors that benefit all people.

Conscious Goal Orientation

Goal setting and goal-oriented behavior are important elements of individual psychology. To understand the behaviors of individuals, one has to become familiar with the **unique goals** they have chosen. The life-style of every individual is contained in this pattern of self-selected goals; it is closely related to the person's creative self. Adler ascribed great importance to the **conscious dimension** of personality and linked the **unconscious** with neurotic behavior: "It is only the unconscious guiding idea of personality that makes the complete neurotic system possible" (Adler, 1955, p. 230).

Birth Order

Adler considered the birth order of siblings in a family an **indicator** of their future attitudes and **behavior patterns.** Oldest, middle, and youngest children allegedly have typical personality characteristics etched by their family constellation.

DEVELOPMENT OF PERSONALITY

When Adler had his private practice in the district of the Prater, a large park and center of popular entertainment, many of his patients were acrobats who performed in the midway area of the park. He noticed that their apparent physical strength was frequently a **compensation** for some other weakness in the organism. This led him to his research into **organ inferiority**, which he later incorporated in his theory of personality.

Feelings of Inferiority

When a child is born, it suffers from feelings of weakness. Adler (1955) emphasized "that the possession of inherited inferior organs, organic systems, and glands with internal secretion created a situation in the early stages of a child's development, **whereby a normal feeling of weakness and helplessness had been enormously intensified and had grown into a deeply felt sense of inferiority**" (p. 18).

Although the feelings of inferiority are a psychological phenomenon, their **cause is physiological**—the weakness of the child's body. According to cultural traditions of his time, Adler equated weakness with femininity or lack of manly vigor. To overcome that weakness, he postulated a compensatory process, which he called **masculine protest.** He later changed this term to **will to power** and eventually to **striving for superiority.**

Adler identified the inferiority feelings in the child as a **minus situation** and extended the validity of this concept to a person's entire life span. He perceived it as the fundamental motivational factor found in every human accomplishment. Without the minus situation a person's life would be stagnant:

> The minus situation is at the basis of any psychological form of expression. Guided by the individual goal of completion, it gives the impetus to progression.... In the end, all great accomplishments stem from the blessed struggle with the needs of childhood. (Adler, 1964, pp. 53–54)

Striving for Superiority

The individual experiences a strong determination to transform the minus situation into a **plus situation** by striving for superiority. There are many concrete forms of doing so: some healthy, others unhealthy. No matter which form the struggle for superiority may assume, Adler (1955) emphasized a fundamental assumption "that the psyche has as its objective the **goal of superiority**" (p. 7).

This striving will, indeed, transform the individual's situation, but the plus sign that replaces the inferiority feelings can have either **healthy** or **unhealthy** connotations. In its healthy form superiority is identical with personality growth and self-actualization. In its unhealthy form it is marked by regressive patterns.

Selfish Striving for Superiority

Adler (1955) warned that striving for superiority was no panacea in itself. Selfish attempts to struggle for power or **antisocial** striving for superiority leads to maladjustment, hypersensitivity, intolerance, and ultimately to a desire "singly to defy the whole world" (p. 68).

Since Adler believed that by age five a child has reached "a unified and crystallized pattern of behavior," it follows that selfish striving for superiority has its beginnings early in childhood. Adler (1958) offered examples of such maladaptive children's profiles. One is the **pampered child:** "He is granted prominence without working to deserve it and he will generally come to feel this prominence as a birth right.... His interest was devoted to himself and he never learned the use and the necessity of cooperation" (p. 16).

When pampered children grow up and encounter typical life problems, they feel ill-treated and abused. They want to have all their demands met, using hostility outright or hiding it behind a facade of good will. In either case, they tyrannize their fellow men.

Another example of maladaptive childhood experiences occurs in the case of the **neglected** or **unwanted child** (Adler, 1958, 1963). Such children have not learned cooperation and have not experienced love. They perceive life as essentially negative, have no confidence in society and do not expect to win affection or esteem by helping others. They are basically suspicious and do not even trust themselves (see Fig. 4).

GOAL OF PERSONALITY DEVELOPMENT: SOCIAL INTEREST

In Adler's view the well-adjusted personality profile is also formed in childhood. The essential mark of a **well-adjusted person** is social interest. At times, Adler's (1964) definition of social interest has been couched in

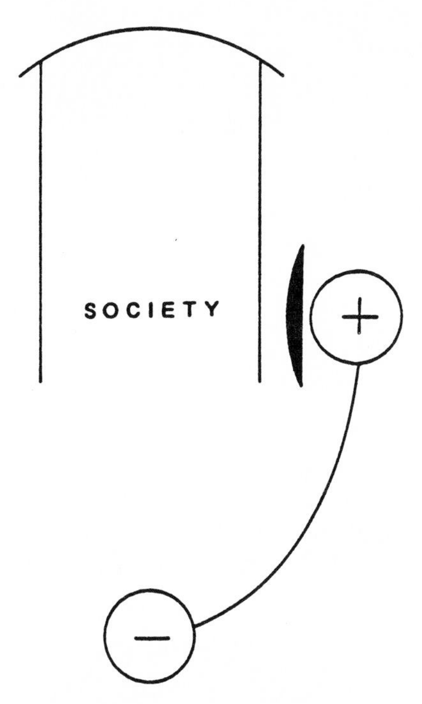

Figure 4. Antisocial striving for superiority. The individual becomes intentionally separated from society.

measured, indirect terms: "to see with the eyes of another, to hear with the ears of another, to feel with the heart of another" (p. 42).

At other times, Adler (1958) defined social interest in concrete terms—as **cooperation** of the individual with others. He did so by referring to his psychiatric practice: "All my efforts are devoted towards increasing the social interest of a patient. I know that the real reason for his malady is his lack of cooperation and I want him to see it too. As soon as he can connect himself with his fellow men on an equal and cooperative footing, he is cured" (p. 260).

It is the **child's mother** who plays a vital role in laying the foundation for the child's social relatedness: "The first task of a mother is to give her child the experience of a trustworthy other person; later she must widen and enlarge this feeling of trust until it includes the rest of the child's environment" (Adler, 1958, pp. 17–18). The full strength of social interest develops out of relationships with playmates and participation in groups of teenage peers; it matures in adult cooperation with coworkers and members of the community (see Fig. 5).

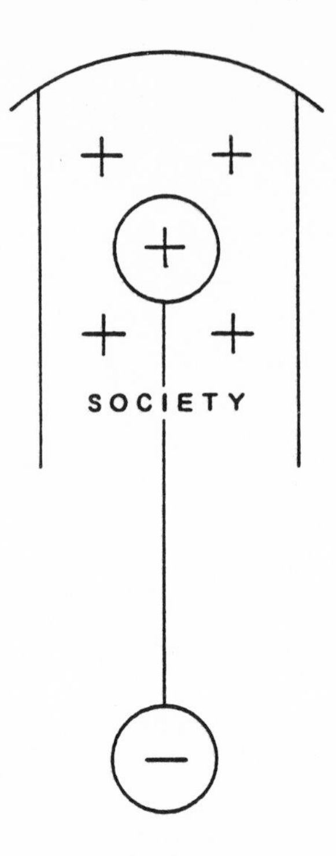

Figure 5. Healthy striving for superiority: Attainment of social interest, mutuality of sharing.

INDIVIDUAL LIFE-STYLE

As may be assumed from the term **individual psychology,** the concept of an individual life-style is central to Adler's theory. It includes **characteristics, traits,** and **behaviors** that express the compensatory attempts, which the person used to overcome feelings of inferiority and to strive for superiority. Also, the **family environment** is seen as influential in molding the individual life-style. Adler (1958) has expressed his belief that life-style significantly affects both the psychic and the somatic elements of the person: "A courageous individual will show the effects of his attitude in his physique. His body will be differently built" (p. 43). We may question, of course, whether courage by itself can influence the structure of one's body, but that is besides the point. Adler wants to underscore his emphasis on a close **psychosomatic relationship** that develops in a fully integrated person.

As individuals plan their future life, they are not primarily influenced by their childhood experiences (as Freud asserted) but by their subjective expectations, which are frequently quite unrealistic. This is particularly true of children and youth but may also apply to adults.

Adler (1956) offers the concept of **fictional finalism** to explain this phenomenon. He admits that many goals that people set for themselves are fictional, but he considers them useful since they provide a **unified pattern of striving** to a person who otherwise may be floundering. Fictional goal patterns, such as "Through honesty I will become wealthy" or "If I will tell the truth, everybody will like me" may not lead to the envisioned outcomes; nevertheless, they may help a child successfully pass through teenage and attain a rewarding life style in adulthood.

THE CREATIVE SELF

In psychological literature the concept of the creative self is often viewed in ambiguous terms or shrouded by a supernatural aura of mysticism (Maddi, 1968). Such interpretations appear, however, rather non-Adlerian in character. It seems preferable to perceive the creative self as an **outgrowth of a positive, healthy life-style.** All persons can uniquely mold their own lives and in the process exert strong influence on their environment.

There are many areas of life that require firm and imaginative interventions of the creative self. One of them is the ongoing need for reconciling the person's individuality and uniqueness with his or her socially oriented, cooperative attitude. The creative self has a special task in promoting the welfare of all mankind. Adler (1964) had a vision of a new society, in which the individual would pursue personal goals fully congruent with the advancement of mankind: "Never can the individual be the goal of the ideal of perfection, but only mankind as a **cooperating community**" (p. 40). There was indeed, a dose of **messianic ardor** in Adler's deeply felt convictions.

BIRTH ORDER

The need for early socialization processes in the family is, in Adler's view, closely tied to the birth order of siblings.

First-born children have the disadvantage of having to leave center stage of parental attention when the second child arrives. If they can be prepared for the arrival of their brother or sister, they can grow through the experience. If, however, the second child is born too close to the first, the first-born **suffers emotionally,** "feels pushed into the background," and becomes alienated from mother. "The child trains himself for isolation" (Adler, 1958, p. 147).

Second or middle-born children are born into a socially balanced situation, sharing mother's attention with one or more siblings, and do not experience the trauma of being dislodged from center stage. An older brother or sister is a stimulus for more **earnest efforts** to succeed. "A typical second child is very easy to recognize. He behaves as if he were in a race, as if someone were a step or two in front and he had to hurry to get ahead of him" (Adler, 1958, p. 148).

Youngest children are usually pampered and, as earlier mentioned, have difficulty in developing social interest. In Adler's view, the oldest and the youngest children have the greatest potential for **maladjustment.**

It needs to be pointed out that major differences exist between the structure of Viennese society in Adler's time and modern society. Whereas at the beginning of the century women in Vienna considered it normal to have children close together, modern women typically space the birth of their children. This means that today we need to apply Adler's birth order theory with a dose of caution.

APPLICATIONS TO COUNSELING

Adler's theory has found numerous applications both in Adlerian counseling and in Reality Therapy, which uses some of its principles. Among particularly useful concepts are the following:

1. Social interest involving (a) personal fulfillment through positive social interactions and (b) priority of cooperation over competition
2. Upbringing of children by parents (or teachers) that would promote trust in the parents (or teachers) and society in general but would avoid pampering the child
3. Emphasis on conscious goal orientation (this emphasis of Adler has been operationally applied in Reality Therapy)
4. Compensation of weakness in one area by striving for excellence in another
5. Acceptance of life's challenges
6. Birth order of siblings for (judicious) interpretation of their behavior

CHAPTER REVIEW

1. Which events in Adler's life were of greatest interest to you?
2. How did Marxist socialism influence Adler's thinking and personal life?
3. What are the main points of Adler's personality theory?
4. How do you define Adler's concept of feelings of inferiority?
5. What is meant by striving for superiority?
6. What is selfish striving for superiority, and what are its origins in the child's upbringing?
7. How does Adler explain his concept of social interest?
8. How can a parent help a child develop social interest?
9. What is meant by individual life-style and by fictional finalism?
10. What is the creative self, and how does it influence the person and the environment?
11. What are Adler's views on the birth order of siblings?
12. Which of Adler's ideas can today's counselors incorporate in their professional work?

REFERENCES

Adler, A. (1956). *The individual psychology of Alfred Adler: A systematic presentation in selections from his writings.* H. L. Ansbacher & R. R. Ansbacher (Eds.). New York: Basic Books.

Adler, A. (1955). *The practice and theory of individual psychology.* London: Routledge & Kegan Paul.

Adler, A. (1963). *The problem child.* New York: Capricorn Books.

Adler, A. (1964). *Superiority and the social interest.* Evanston, IL: Northwestern University Press.

Adler, A. (1958). *What life should mean to you.* New York: Capricorn Books.

Bottome, P. (1939). *Alfred Adler.* London: Faber & Faber.

Brome, V. (1967). *Freud and his early circle: The struggle of psycho-analysis.* London: Heinemann.

Maddi, S. (1968). *Personality theories: A comparative analysis.* Homewood, IL: Dorsey Press.

CHAPTER 5

INTERPERSONAL THEORIES

THE INTERPERSONAL theories of Karen Horney and Harry Stack Sullivan are building on the pioneering work of Alfred Adler. He broke away from Freud's overriding emphasis on intrapsychic processes in personal development. Instead of accepting instinctual forces as the primary determinants of behavior, Adler pointed out the role of social elements in every individual's growth. Social interest, manifested through cooperative striving, was in his view every person's ultimate self-fulfillment.

Horney and Sullivan offer two distinct theories, which suggest concrete steps that individuals can take to attain the goal of social relatedness proposed by Adler. The differences of Horney's and Sullivan's approaches have resulted both from their varied theoretical backgrounds and from the contrasting cultural influences that molded their lives. Horney came to the United States from Germany, where she received a typical European university education and also absorbed the principles of classical psychoanalysis. Sullivan was American-born with a pragmatic bent typical of his culture. He was less exposed to psychoanalytic training than Horney and had no qualms about using unconventional approaches or developing his unusual terminology.

KAREN HORNEY (1885-1952)

Karen Horney was born in the north German city of Hamburg. Her father, a sea captain, was relatively old and often stern. Her mother, 17 years younger than her husband, was an intelligent and highly cultured woman. Karen was much closer to her mother. In her diary, Horney (1980) vividly recounted episodes from the upper middle-class family and from her student days in a convent school. She also confessed her crushes on various teachers and her inner religious struggles about the meaning of biblical teachings. After graduation from the gymnasium, she entered, at the urging of her mother, medical school, where she gained the respect of her male classmates by her intelligence and friendliness. In later entries in the diary, Horney candidly discussed her erotic attractions to various men. Eventually, she married Oskar Horney, a lawyer and economist, whom she met during her university years. The marriage eventually ended in divorce.

Horney underwent psychoanalytic training in Berlin and was analyzed by two close associates of Freud, Karl Abraham and Hans Sachs. During this period, she experienced intervals of severe physical exhaustion, which baffled and depressed her. She wrote, "When I waken in the morning, I wish the day were already over . . . and I do so passionately want to be active" (Horney, 1980, pp. 270–271).

After a four-year teaching assignment at the Berlin Psychoanalytic Institute, Horney came to the United States and was engaged in clinical work, first in Chicago and later in New York, where she also taught at the American Psychoanalytic Institute. During this period, her disenchantment with classical psychoanalysis became quite pronounced, and she eventually resigned her teaching position. During her psychiatric practice in the United States, Horney noted major differences in the kinds of neuroses of her American and European patients. This insight reinforced her conviction that social values and the culture of a country played a major role in shaping one's personality, both in its healthy and pathological aspects.

Horney made many contributions to her professional field. In a low-key but effective manner, she promoted understanding of the psychology of women and furthered their social equality. She rejected Freud's idea of an inherent physiological inferiority that manifests itself in women through penis envy, and pointed out that passive and often subservient attitudes of women are the result of long-term social and cultural influences.

MAIN EMPHASIS IN HORNEY'S THEORY

Horney followed the psychoanalytical tradition by ascribing a major role in personality development to **childhood experiences.** Freud linked experiences of the infant with pressures of instinctual drives. Adler postulated physiological weakness as the source of the child's feelings of inferiority. By contrast, Horney's concept of basic anxiety was rooted in **social factors** of the child's environment.

Horney developed a theoretical framework for helping children overcome their basic anxiety and adults their neurotic needs. In all her writings she combined **elements of psychoanalysis** with a strong **social orientation.**

THE CHILD'S BASIC ANXIETY

In Horney's view, children have been born into a problem-laden world. Childhood anxiety is not self-generated; it is caused by adults who are "wrapped up in their own neuroses" and display unpredictable behavior: "In simple words, they may be dominating, overprotective, intimidating, irritable, overexacting, overindulgent, erratic, partial to other siblings, hypocritical, indifferent, etc." (Horney, 1950, p. 18).

The more a child is exposed to such adverse factors in the environment, particularly in the family, the more insecurity it will experience. Horney (1945) called special attention to

> the child's sense of lurking hypocrisy in the environment: his feeling that the parents' love, their Christian charity, honesty, generosity, and so on may be only pretense. Part of what the child feels on this score is really hypocrisy; but some of it may be just his reaction to all the contradictions he senses in the parents' behavior. (pp. 41–42.)

The seemingly endless stream of contradictory messages from the adult world confuses the child and makes him or her feel helpless and isolated. The child feels insecure, becomes overly sensitive, and is easily hurt (Horney, 1937, 1945). Instead of developing a sense of belonging, the child is overcome by basic anxiety, which Horney (1950) defined "as a feeling of being isolated and helpless toward a world potentially hostile" (p. 366).

RELATIONSHIPS WITH OTHERS

To overcome basic anxiety and attain a degree of security, the child employs various interpersonal relationships. Horney (1945) classified these relationships according to three categories: (1) moving toward people, (2) moving against people, and (3) moving away from people (see Fig. 6).

1. When moving **toward people,** usually family members, the child tries to obtain their good will, to depend on them, and thus to assure personal safety. If there is discord among the adults, the child will cling to the person who appears to be strongest.

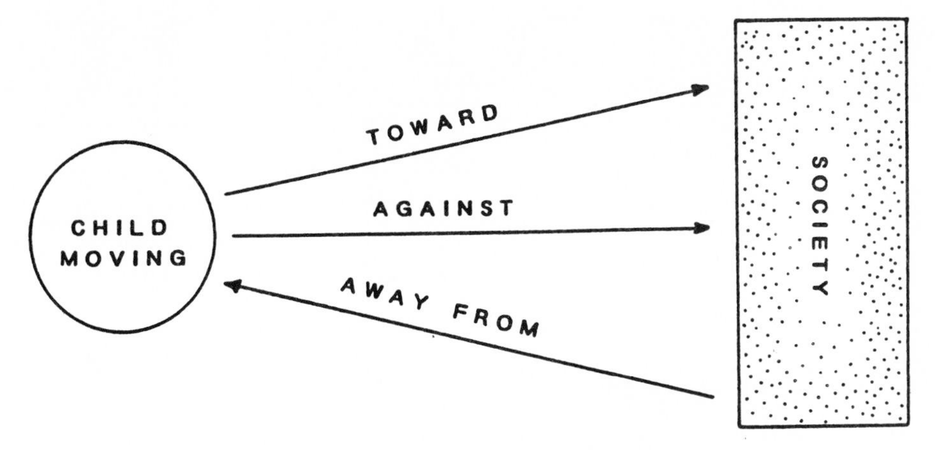

Figure 6. Three ways in which a child can relate to others in society.

2. The child who moves **against people** expresses distrust towards society. He or she has come to the conclusion that aggressive behavior is the only means for survival. The child wants to get the upper hand and to defeat others. (This idea of Horney parallels Adler's view of the child who seeks power.)
3. Finally, the child who moves **away from people** neither wants to belong nor to fight others. The child withdraws from relating to others since most people don't seem to understand or care. This can often be done in an acceptable way. Children who have their minds set only on school books but avoid peer contacts are an example of this kind of behavior.

The **highly threatened child** will rigidly adhere to only one of the three ways of dealing with others. If, for instance, moving against others seems to be the most effective coping behavior, the child will be consistently and uncontrollably aggressive. If moving towards others works best, the child's affection will turn into blind adherence and conformism. If moving away from others offers good results, the child's legitimate need for privacy will develop into an avoidance of all human relationships.

Mental health is found only in a natural, free-flowing combination of the three ways of relating to others, depending on various life situations:

> In a healthy human relationship the moves toward, against, or away from others are not mutually exclusive. The ability to want and to give affection, or to give in; the ability to fight, and the ability to keep to oneself—these are complementary capacities necessary for good human relations. But in the child who feels himself on precarious ground because of his basic anxiety,

> these moves become extreme and rigid. Affection, for instance, becomes clinging; compliance becomes appeasement. Similarly, he is driven to rebel or to keep aloof. (Horney, 1950, p. 19.)

NEUROTIC NEEDS OF ADULTS

In Horney's view, neurotic needs that appear in adulthood are merely extensions of rigid, maladaptive social attitudes in childhood. For instance, an adult, who suffers from the neurotic need for approval and affection, is likely to have adhered to a pattern of always pleasing people in childhood—moving toward them—and avoiding even minor disagreements.

Horney (1942) pointed out that adult neurotic needs are marked by **compulsiveness** and that their essential elements are **unconscious.** The individual is driven to a particular behavior, does not fully understand its meaning, or may not interpret it correctly. She list ten neurotic needs, but adds that the list is neither complete nor clear-cut. Other needs may have to be added as society develops new interests and behaviors. Horney's (1942) originally proposed neurotic needs are as follows:

1. The neurotic need for affection and approval
2. The neurotic need for a "partner" who will take over one's life
3. The neurotic need to restrict one's life within narrow borders
4. The neurotic need for power
5. The neurotic need to exploit others
6. The neurotic need for prestige
7. The neurotic need for personal admiration
8. The neurotic need for personal achievement
9. The neurotic need for self-sufficiency and independence
10. The neurotic need for perfection and unassailability

Overcoming Neuroticism

Although fully recognizing the value of psychotherapy for most patients, Horney (1950) emphasized the need for self-help in the field of mental illness. She assumed many curative forces to be embedded in the mind of every maladjusted person and considered life itself to be a curative process offering countless opportunities for personality change. Examples of significant persons in one's life may stimulate such a change, or a shared tragedy may help the neurotic break out of isolation and discover that other people possess caring attitudes.

APPLICATIONS TO COUNSELING

Horney's theory of personality presents elements that may find direct application in counseling practice:

1. The concept of basic anxiety
2. The need for even-tempered, straightforward parental attitudes in dealing with children
3. The three ways of relating to others
4. The neurotic needs of adults
5. Ways of remediating emotional problems

HARRY STACK SULLIVAN (1892–1949)

Harry Stack Sullivan was born of Irish ancestry on a farm in New York State. His family was poor and felt ostracized by many of its "Yankee neighbors." Young Harry had few childhood friends and often suffered from loneliness. After high school he was admitted to the Chicago College of Medicine and Surgery from which he graduated in 1917. He had some exposure to Freud's ideas during his studies and underwent about 75 hours of psychoanalysis. After graduation he served in the army and later became a medical officer and consultant in various government agencies. He was on the staff of hospitals in Washington, D.C. and taught at the University of Maryland.

Sullivan was a prolific lecturer; his taped lectures and notes that were later published comprise a significant part of his theoretical legacy. He had close contacts with a number of social scientists and became involved in various field projects, for instance, a study of the lives of blacks in the South. Another interest of his was the publishing field of psychiatric journals. Sullivan eventually assumed the stature of a statesman in the psychiatric profession and after World War II became involved in working with UNESCO and the World Health Organization. He died in 1949 during a professional trip to Europe.

POINTS OF EMPHASIS IN SULLIVAN'S THEORY

Concept of Personality

Unlike the theorists covered so far, Sullivan does not perceive personality as real by itself; it is merely **an inference of interpersonal relationships.** These interpersonal relationships begin in infancy and last throughout the life span of a person. The interpersonal dimension of human life is the foundation of Sullivan's personality concept.

Personality Adjustment: Social, Sexual, and Cognitive

In Sullivan's view, the development of personal maturity and self-fulfillment requires the combination of appropriate developmental processes in the **social, sexual, and cognitive** domains. Unless each of the three areas of life has reached its appropriate level of development, personality adjustment will not occur.

Stages of Development

Sullivan perceived the development of personality as occurring in stages. His emphasis on stages and on the sexual dimension of personality **resembles elements of Freud's theory.**

Nipple-In-Lips Theory

Sullivan's major contribution to the understanding of interpersonal relationships is his nipple-in-lips theory. He considered breast feeding to be the **first interpersonal experience** of the infant.

SULLIVAN'S TERMINOLOGY AND BASIC CONCEPTS

Since Sullivan used his own terminology for the innovative concepts that he developed, an explanation of these concepts will be presented, along with a glossary of Sullivan's terminology.

Dynamisms

Sullivan's theory assigns an important role to the concept of dynamisms. A dynamism may be perceived as a basic building unit of the interpersonal dimension of personality—a **pattern of energy transformation.** Interpersonal relationships involve numerous dynamisms. The **dynamism of lust** is Sullivan's (1953) term for instinctual drives—"certain tensions of or pertaining to genitals" (p. 109).

The Nipple-in-Lips Phenomenon

Sullivan considered breast- (or bottle-) feeding to be the first significant interpersonal contact of the infant with society. The infant attains the strongest interpersonal experience through direct contact of its oral zone with the nipple of the mother (Sullivan calls the nursing person "the mothering one"). To a lesser degree, such experience is provided by means of bottle-feeding that may provide clues to the mother's emotional state.

Sullivan (1953) postulated four situations that the infant may encounter in breast-feeding. I am listing only two of these situations, which are most significant. The first affects mostly the **oral zone;** the second has an impact on the infant's **emotional state:** (1) "The good and satisfactory nipple in lips which is the signal—the uncomplicated signal for nursing" and (2) "The evil nipple, the nipple of an anxious mother" (p. 80) that generates tension in the infant. Sullivan emphasized that, because of the emotional state of the mother, the feeding process can have either beneficial or potentially harmful effects on the child's interpersonal development.

Development of Cognition

Sullivan postulated three developmental modes of cognition:

1. The newly born infant has **prototaxic** cognition. Sullivan (1953) explained it as a "series of momentary states of the sensitive organism, with special reference to the zones of interaction with the environment" (p. 29). This includes tactile, visual, and auditory perceptions.
2. **Parataxic** cognition is the second developmental mode; it helps the child discover certain relationships of events although not always in a logical manner. For instance, a small piece of wood that mother threw in the pond floats. Her wristwatch, however, which was even

smaller, sank to the bottom when her child, influenced by parataxic thought processes, tossed it in the pond. Parataxic thought is often present even in adults and manifests itself particularly through superstitious or other irrational behavior.

3. **Syntaxic** cognition is identical with full reasoning and logical judgments that are typical of more mature children and adults.

Tension

Sullivan postulated two opposite states that he called **absolute euphoria** and **absolute tension,** the latter also termed **terror.** The individual has a tendency to approximate, whenever possible, the state of euphoria. In reality, however, at least moderate tension is the prevalent psychological state of most people. Tension can be generated by **neglected needs** of the organism or by **anxiety.** Long-lasting neglect of needs produces **apathy,** a lackadaisical state, "by which personality in utter fiasco rests until it can do something else" (Sullivan, 1970, p. 184). Prolonged anxiety-related tension leads to **somnolent detachment;** an infant falls asleep, and an adult may induce sleep artificially by the use of drugs (see Fig. 7).

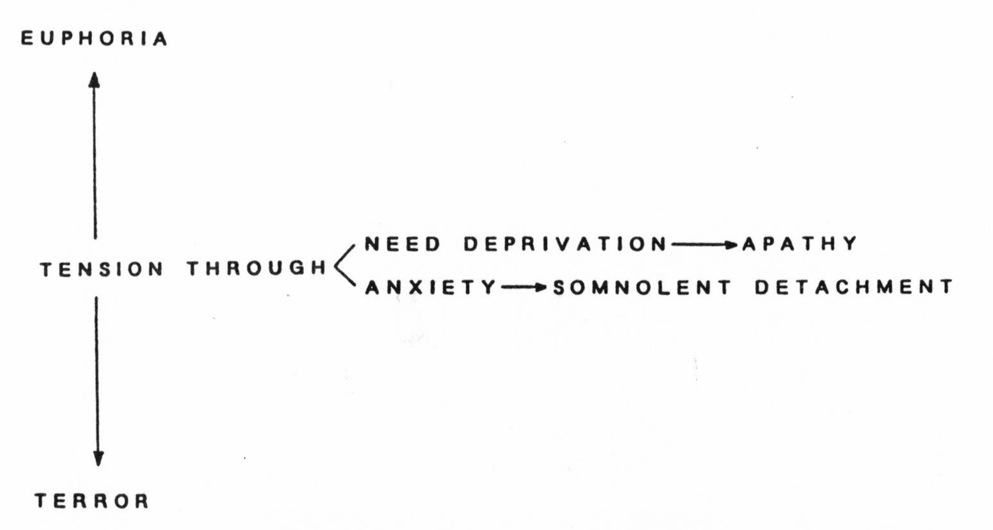

Figure 7. Diagram of tension in Sullivan's theory.

Self-System and Sublimation

The previous explanation of tension is based on Sullivan's view that every person naturally desires the fulfillment of two concerns that frequently work at cross-purposes. They are **need satisfaction** and **interpersonal security**, the opposite of **anxiety**. While the child attempts to satisfy its real or imaginary needs, it often triggers negative responses from adults. To escape such unpleasant situations, when they occur, the child learns to employ the **self-system**, a dynamism that helps develop "general skills to avoid forbidding gestures and . . . verbal techniques for putting a somewhat better face on difficult situations" (Sullivan, 1953, p. 101).

To prevent such situations from occurring, the child learns to employ a related dynamism that Sullivan calls **sublimation.** In contrast to psychoanalysis, however, he perceives the term in a broader than strictly sexual context. In his view, it is the substitution "of a socially more acceptable activity pattern which satisfies parts of the motivational system that caused trouble" (Sullivan, 1953, p. 193).

Thus, we can conclude that the two dynamisms—the self-system and sublimation: (1) have a common purpose of helping the child deal with anxiety through positive interpersonal relationships; (2) differ from each other by the means they apply for achieving that purpose.

Personifications

The child makes an initial differentiation between self and all that is external and concurrently forms images of self and the environment. This is the process of personification involving "**me**" and "**not me.**" Additionally, the "me" is evaluated by the child on the basis of interpersonal relationships with significant others. The result is an additional personification of the "**good me**" or the "**bad me.**"

Malevolent Transformation

Malevolent transformation is Sullivan's term for the disappointment and the resulting **angry reaction of the child** who longs for tenderness but is repeatedly denied tender care by adults. The child may have received tender treatment in earlier years. Now, he or she is made anxious by the lack of concern on the part of adults. As a result, the child reacts to friendly approaches by strangers with a degree of hostility.

STAGES OF PERSONALITY DEVELOPMENT

Sullivan postulated six stages between birth and late adolescence in which the social, sexual, and cognitive development of personality occurs. Each stage contains a number of the dynamic processes explained in the previous section.

1. **Infancy** (from birth to the development of articulate speech). The infant has nipple-in-lips experiences and is subjected to tension that may lead to apathy or somnolent detachment. Personifications develop, and the infant acquires full body awareness. The initial prototaxic cognition mode changes into parataxic cognition around the end of this stage.

2. **Childhood** (lasting until kindergarten or first grade). The child has a need for playmates. Differentiation of masculine and feminine roles occurs. At times, the child uses the mechanism of malevolent transformation. To avoid anxiety, the child learns how to use the self-system and begins to employ preventive strategies of sublimation. Gradually, syntaxic cognition appears.

3. **Juvenile era** (coincides with early elementary school years). The child is being increasingly socialized, mostly through group interaction. Attitudes are forming, and sublimation becomes more effective.

4. **Preadolescence** (lasting about a year or two). The child has a need for a peer of the same sex—called "chum" by Sullivan. The chum is the child's best friend and "matters even when he isn't there" (Sullivan, 1970, p. 144).

5. **Early adolescence** (characterized by emerging heterosexual interests). This is the era of youthful eroticism. A boy, for instance, "begins to feel that one of the girls is far more attractive than he has previously noticed" (Sullivan, 1970, p. 146).

6. **Late adolescence** (young adulthood). The youth "begins late adolescence when he discovers what he likes in the way of genital behavior and how to fit it into the rest of life" (Sullivan, 1953, p. 297). In contrast to Freud, Sullivan emphasized that the **dynamism of lust** had to be **combined with the need for intimacy** to form a sociosexual integration.

Through the stages of this developmental process, a broad repertory of interpersonal relationships has been formed and an appropriate understanding of personal duties, privileges, and responsibilities has gradually emerged. The young person has now attained a relative degree of maturity in the three important areas of life—**social, sexual,** and **cognitive.**

APPLICATIONS TO COUNSELING

Sullivan (1970) proposed a systematic interviewing process for helping professionals. Although his psychiatric orientation of interviewing may find less acceptance among counselors, the personality theory offers several useful elements for the counseling practice:

1. The gradual process of personality development in youth
2. The nipple-in-lips theory, which underscores the importance of parental attitudes for the psychological development of the child in early infancy
3. The linkage of social and sexual dynamics
4. The concept of tension and its effects on the individual
5. The insight into early cognitive processes

CHAPTER REVIEW

1. When reading Horney's life story, what impressed you most?
2. What is the main emphasis of Horney's theory?
3. What are the causes of a child's basic anxiety?
4. Which three directional moves does Horney perceive as ways for the child to relate to society?
5. What is for her the indicator of a child's mental health or maladjustment?
6. How does Horney explain the neurotic needs in adults?
7. Which events do you remember from Sullivan's life?
8. What is Sullivan's concept of personality and what are the three components of personality adjustment?
9. What is meant by the concept of dynamism, and how does Sullivan define the dynamism of lust?
10. What does Sullivan imply by his nipple-in-lips theory?
11. Which three stages of cognitive development does he postulate?
12. How does Sullivan perceive tension, and what are the outcomes of long-term tension?
13. What is meant by the processes of personification and malevolent transformation?
14. Which stages of personality development does Sullivan envision?
15. Which ideas of Horney or Sullivan seem useful to you for today's counseling practice?

REFERENCES

Horney, K. (1980). *The adolescent diaries of Karen Horney.* New York: Basic Books.
Horney, K. (1950). *Neurosis and human growth.* New York: Norton.
Horney, K. (1937). *The neurotic personality of our time.* New York: Norton.
Horney, K. (1945). *Our inner conflicts.* New York: Norton.
Horney, K. (1942). *Self-analysis.* New York: Norton.
Sullivan, H. S. (1953). *The interpersonal theory of psychiatry.* New York: Norton.
Sullivan, H. S. (1970). *The psychiatric interview.* New York: Norton.

CHAPTER 6

PSYCHOSOCIAL THEORIES

PSYCHOLOGICAL literature uses a variety of classifications for the personality theories discussed in Chapters 4 through 6 of this volume. The same theory may be labeled social-psychological, neo-Freudian, analytic, or sociocultural.

In my judgment, Adler's theory, because of its new social emphasis in personality development, deserved a detailed explanation, particularly since other theorists followed Adler's leadership. Horney and Sullivan show a commonality of purpose in their work. They clarify, each in a unique way, the specific roles that interpersonal relationships have in the shaping of personality. Likewise, Fromm and Erikson share mutual characteristics—(1) a post-Freudian orientation and (2) an interest in sociocultural factors that influence personality adjustment. Their theories are viewed here as "psychosocial." This term was used by Erikson himself to identify the nature of his theory.

ERICH FROMM (1900-1980)

Erich Fromm was born in Frankfurt of orthodox Jewish parents. As a young boy he experienced the sting of anti-Semitic attitudes prevalent among Germans of various Christian faiths and also the clannishness of Jewish people. Early in life he became interested in psychology, which he chose as his major field of studies at the university while maintaining an interest in philosophy and sociology. He earned his doctoral degree in psychology at the University of Heidelberg.

As a young man he began reading Marx and Freud and was greatly influenced by their ideas. He tried to develop a synthesis of the two theories, using the social concepts of Marx as a general framework and supplying needed psychological elements from Freud's work. Although his interest in Marxist socialism remained strong through his life, he preferred to be called a "dialectic humanist" rather than a Marxian theorist.

Fromm received formal psychoanalytic training in Munich and Berlin, where he became acquainted with Karen Horney. For the first years of his career as analyst, he followed the classical approach of Freud in treating patients. Eventually, he adjusted his views and substantially deviated from classical psychoanalytic theory. Nevertheless, he always considered himself to be a pupil of Freud who was merely "attempting to bring out [Freud's] most important discoveries in order to enrich and deepen them by liberating them from the somewhat narrow libido theory" (Fromm, 1966, p. 59).

After his emigration to the United States in the early 1930s, he went for a short time to Chicago before settling in New York. He became associated with various institutions of higher learning in the area, particularly with the American Institute of Psychoanalysis, where he accepted a teaching position. There he met again Karen Horney who also taught courses in psychoanalysis. However, this time a serious friction developed between them. Horney objected to Fromm's teaching at the Institute without a medical degree; subsequently, Fromm was restricted in the number of courses he could teach, and he decided to leave. Several of his colleagues resigned in protest.

In 1949, Fromm moved to Mexico to help alleviate the arthritic problems of his wife in the dry climate of Cuernavaca, and he stayed there even after she died. In 1957, he initiated a major research project focusing on the impact of industrialization on Mexican rural society. When he was in his mid-seventies, Fromm moved to Switzerland and remained involved in professional work until his death in 1980.

MAIN EMPHASIS IN FROMM'S THEORY

Fromm was as much a sociologist, historian, and philosopher as he was a psychologist. Since he perceived the lives of individuals in a global perspective of **society**, he was often critical of the pathogenic, dehumanizing influences of modern culture on people. He tried to counteract this negative impact by making people aware of their selfhood and inner worth.

Although freedom is essential to human nature, many people are unwilling to use it and thus pave the way for dictatorial systems. To assert one's **freedom**, every person needs to make value choices, develop a productive orientation, and discover the beauty and power or caring attitudes (Fromm, 1962, 1969).

Fromm's Marxian bent is evident from the choice between "robotism" and "humanistic communitarian socialism" that he viewed as the prevalent issue in modern society. He defined humanistic communitarian **socialism** as a system "in which every working person would be an active and responsible participant, where work would be attractive and meaningful, where capital would not employ labor, but labor would employ capital" (Fromm, 1955, p. 248). This concept of Fromm parallels Adler's vision of society as a "cooperating community."

THE CONCEPT OF PERSONALITY

Fromm (1947) defined personality as "the totality of inherited and acquired psychic qualities which are characteristic of one individual and which make the individual unique" (p. 59).

He differentiated two components of personality—**temperament** and **character:**

> The difference between inherited and acquired qualities is on the whole synonymous with the difference between temperament, gifts, and all constitutionally given psychic qualities on the one hand and character on the other. While differences in temperament have no ethical significance, differences in character constitute the real problem of ethics; they are expressive of the degree to which an individual has succeeded in the art of living. (Fromm, 1947, p. 59.)

Temperament is the basic tool of personality, **constitutional** in nature and fairly permanent. Character, however, is formed according to **value choices** of the individual modified by sociocultural influences in the environment.

PRODUCTIVE AND NONPRODUCTIVE CHARACTER

According to Fromm, personality adjustment is achieved in the domain of a person's character. In describing the various blends of character orientations, Fromm (1947) recognizes two basic patters that typically exist in every individual, side by side. They are:

1. the **productive character,** which concentrates on giving to others through love and work: "One loves that for which one labors, and one labors for that which one loves" (Fromm, 1947, p. 99).

2. the **nonproductive character** which is based on the assumption that one is unable to produce and thus has to receive from others what he or

she needs; this can happen either by one's passive behavior or by some active effort, e.g., exploitation.

Two basic processes underlie the nature of both character patterns: (1) one is **socialization**, by which a person relates to others and oneself and is willing to offer care; (2) the other is **assimilation**, by which one acquires or assimilates desired objects. It is evident that socialization is closely linked with traits of the productive character, whereas assimilation promotes the nonproductive character orientation. A well-adjusted person possesses a character based on a fairly permanent pattern, in which the two processes have been properly blended.

Fromm described the productive character orientation in these terms:

> An active person, not only in physical work but also in feeling, in thinking, in his relationships with people. He approaches the world as the possessor in an active manner, and all the expressions of his being are authentic; that is, they are genuinely his, and are not put into him by an outside influence, such as a newspaper or a movie. (Evans, 1966, p. 15.)

The productive and nonproductive orientations are interlocked within every person's psyche. If the productive orientation is predominant, the nonproductive character modalities listed below lose their negative connotations and become growth-promoting.

Under the heading "Nonproductive Orientations," Fromm (1947) listed four modalities:

1. The **receptive orientation.** A person with this orientation expects all material and psychological support from external sources.
2. The **exploitative orientation.** A person with this orientation not only expects all support to come from external sources but is also determined to get whatever is needed by grabbing or stealing it. Fromm termed such behavior "essentially cannibalistic."
3. The **hoarding orientation.** A person with this orientation wants to keep accumulated goods, displays social aloofness, and has developed strong defenses against intrusions from the outside world.
4. The **marketing orientation.** A person with this orientation is committed to the principle that everything one needs is generated through the process of exchange. The market provides the final evaluation of things. In addition to traditional marketing, modern society has added a new variation—the personality market. Individuals are not respected for who they are but rather what impression they make. People's personalities are for sale like other commodities:

Success depends largely on how well a person sells himself on the market, how well he gets his personality across, how nice a "package" he is; whether he is "cheerful," "sound," "aggressive," "reliable," "ambitious"; furthermore what his family background is, what clubs he belongs to, and whether he knows the right people. (Fromm, 1947, p. 77.)

HUMAN NEEDS AND LOVE

Fromm (1947) postulated five basic needs in every human being: (1) the need for **relatedness,** (2) the need for **transcendence,** (3) the need for **rootedness,** (4) the need for **identity,** and (5) the need for a **frame of orientation.**

A mature, well-adjusted person is characterized by the ability to integrate these needs, particularly the needs of relatedness and identity. Such a person is capable of intimately relating to another person without loss of identity. The force that fosters relatedness while preserving identity is mature love; it flows from the productive character orientation:

In contrast to symbiotic union, mature **love** is **union under the condition of preserving one's integrity,** one's individuality. **Love is an active power in man;** a power which breaks through the walls, which separate man from his fellow men, which unites him with others; love makes him overcome the sense of isolation and separatedness, yet it permits him to be himself, to retain his integrity. (Fromm, 1962, pp. 20–21.)

Fromm (1950) applied the principle of the healing power of love to therapy, which he defined as "**an attempt to help the patient gain or regain his capacity for love.** If this aim is fulfilled, nothing but surface changes can be accomplished" (p. 87).

APPLICATIONS TO COUNSELING

Fromm proposes several concepts that may be useful in counseling practice, e.g.:

1. Character formation through personal choices
2. The processes of assimilation and socialization that influence character formation
3. The distinction of productive and nonproductive character orientations and specific modalities of the latter
4. The role of mature love (caring) in the therapeutic process

ERIK ERIKSON (1902-1994)

Erik Erikson, although born in Germany, was of Danish ancestry. From his earliest childhood on, he experienced an identity crisis that profoundly influenced his thinking and eventually became a distinguishing mark of his personality theory.

When Erikson reached the 68th year of his life, he disclosed that his birth "was the result of his Lutheran mother's extramarital affair. He never knew his Danish father" (Woodward, 1994, p. 56). A few years later, Erik's mother married the German pediatrician who took care of her child, Doctor Homburger. He was a prosperous Jewish professional, and he decided to adopt Erik. This caring act proved, however, to be of mixed blessing for the boy: his Christian classmates ostracized him as a Jew, while he was disliked by people in the synagogue because of his non-Jewish features—blue eyes and blond hair.

Erik went to school in Karlsruhe and followed a carefully structured curriculum that would prepare him for university studies. After passing the abitur—an exam required for admission to higher education—he decided, however, to forgo university studies and chose instead to wander through Europe in search of his true self. After a year of spontaneous wandering, he made up his mind to become an artist and returned to Karlsruhe to attend art school. His career began in Munich, where he produced mostly woodcuts, drawings, and etchings.

In 1927, he received an invitation from a former high school classmate to come to Vienna and become involved in a unique venture. He was to teach at a private school for children whose parents or who themselves were undergoing analysis with Sigmund Freud. During the years he taught in the school, Erikson was analyzed by Freud's daughter, Anna, an accomplished psychotherapist. He also married Joan Serson, a graduate student from the University of Pennsylvania who was in Europe collecting data for her doctoral dissertation on dance.

After Hitler assumed power in Germany, the Eriksons decided to emigrate, with their two small sons, to America. Erikson became involved in professional work as analyst and researcher, first in the Boston area and later on the West Coast. When he accepted a professorship at the University of California, the fact that he had no formal graduate degree was considered unimportant, because his research and writing were already highly respected. His book, *Childhood and Society,* published in 1950, had a major influence on the thinking of the professional community and the general public. He is also known for his work with Indian tribes in South Dakota and California and for his psychohistorical studies on Luther, Ghandi, Maxim Gorky, and Hitler.

MAIN POINTS OF EMPHASIS IN ERIKSON'S THEORY

Modification of Psychoanalysis

Erikson is a post-Freudian who has successfully applied modified psychoanalytical concepts to life in modern society. He has reduced the importance of instinctual drives in shaping human behavior. In his view, physiological pressures on personality are balanced by sociocultural influences.

Epigenetic Stages of Human Growth

Erikson perceived personality development as proceeding in epigenetic stages from birth to adulthood and old age. He explained the epigenetic principle in his dialogue with Richard Evans (1967): "Epi means upon; and genesis, emergence. So epigenesis means that one item develops on top of another in space and in time, and this seemed to me a simple enough configuration to be adopted for our purposes. But, of course, I extended it to include a hierarchy of stages, not just a sequence" (pp. 21–22).

Identity and Ego

The central issue of Erikson's developmental process is the formation of personal identity, which is closely linked with ego development. A person has to acquire an adequate sense of identity before a mature ego emerges. Erikson believes that rites of puberty and confirmation ceremonies are vehicles for affirming the acquisition of identity and ego integration. His concept of the ego differs from that of Freud: the ego is active both within the psyche and in relation to its social environment (Erikson, 1968).

PERSONALITY DEVELOPMENT

Erikson (1950, 1974) proposed and later additionally clarified his structure of personality development, which he envisions in eight stages. Each stage is presented in the form of a psychological crisis that involves two conflicting polarities. As is true of all crises, Erikson's stages contain potential opportunities for growth and elements of danger.

Growth occurs when the conflict is adequately resolved. The resolution produces a new ego strength, which Erikson (1964) calls **virtue.** The elements of danger lie in the person's avoiding to properly resolve the conflict. If that happens, the negative polarity becomes dominant and the virtue fails to emerge. For instance, in the fourth stage—industry vs. inferiority—the virtue to be generated is competence. Yet, if the conflict has not been adequately resolved, the child leaves the stage with a feeling of inferiority (the negative polarity, which has become dominant) rather than with an inner competence (the virtue, which should have been generated).

Such a negative outcome weakens the ego, and unless the problem is remedied, the person's psychological development will be thwarted. The only way in which the problem can be remedied requires a corrective initiative later on. It would involve retracing one's steps to the point, at which the negative outcome occurred, attacking the unresolved conflict more effectively, and thus generating the missing virtue.

The Eight Stages

1. **Trust vs. basic mistrust.** The infant has a need for nourishment, sound sleep, and unhindered bowel movements. The maternal figure provides security for the infant if her behavior is predictable. The infant learns to trust her and eventually trust him- or herself. This basic trust helps the infant develop effective coping behaviors for teething and other unpleasant episodes in the developmental process. The virtue of this stage is **hope**—a basic human strength, which Erikson views as a condition for staying alive rather than as a philosophical or theological concept.

2. **Autonomy vs. shame and doubt.** The child is engaging in new activities—walking and talking—and is developing bowel control. Erikson emphasized the need for balance between "holding on" and "letting go,"

since the anal-muscular behavior has implications for social interactions: too much rigidity or too few restraints. The virtue of this stage is **will.**

3. **Initiative vs. guilt.** The child plans, experiments with, and gets involved in new activities. Pushing too hard for success in new projects, particularly if the needs of others are being disregarded, will make the child feel guilty. Other guilt feelings may be the result of fantasies, some of them sexual. The virtue of this stage is **purpose:** the child may use play to offer clues to his or her future aspirations.

4. **Industry vs. inferiority.** The child is now moving from play to more productive pursuits involving skills and the appropriate use of tools. Success makes the child happy; failure to succeed stimulates a feeling of inferiority, even if the task was too difficult for the age level of the child. The virtue of this stage is **competence**—a step in the direction of mature task orientation.

5. **Identity vs. role diffusion.** Erikson (1965) believed that "in no other stage of the life cycle . . . are the promise of finding oneself and the threat of losing oneself so closely allied" (p. 11). This stage integrates all previous self-images of the young person. The sense of ego identity is the confidence that one's own self-perception is matched by the perception of others. The virtue of this stage is **fidelity,** a personal commitment to a chosen vocational pattern or philosophy of life.

6. **Intimacy vs. isolation.** In Erikson's view, intimacy is a healthy way of fusing one's identity with the identity of another without fear of losing or diluting oneself. Intimacy should involve commitment and may be expressed sexually. The process of intimacy may help clarify one's own identity through the identification with another person. The virtue of this stage is **love.**

7. **Generativity vs. stagnation.** During this stage people become involved with society for the purpose of generating something of value, be it offspring, material goods, works of art, or creative ideas. The virtue of this stage is **care,** a willingness to make a constructive contribution to society.

8. **Ego integrity vs. despair.** Unless a person can look back in old age at his or her life with a sense of accomplishment and personal fulfillment, despair sets in. Erikson (1950) saw a relation between infantile trust and adult integrity: "Healthy children will not fear life if their parents have integrity enough not to fear death" (p. 133). The virtue of this stage is **wisdom**—the embodiment of the entire developmental cycle of the individual.

APPLICATIONS TO COUNSELING

Erikson offers numerous practical ideas that can be used by counselors today. Among them are:

1. The concept of epigenetic development of personality
2. A detailed analysis of psychosocial processes in childhood
3. The central role of ego identity throughout the life span
4. The view of life as a series of unavoidable conflict situations that need to be resolved
5. The extension of Freud's stages to adulthood and old age

CHAPTER REVIEW

1. What are the highlights of Fromm's life?
2. What do you perceive as the main emphasis of Fromm's personality theory?
3. In Fromm's view, personality is composed of two factors. What are they?
4. What processes underlie the formation of a person's character?
5. Can you define the productive character orientation and the four main modalities of the nonproductive orientation?
6. Which human needs, in Fromm's view, can be reconciled only through mature love?
7. What interested you in Erikson's biography?
8. Which are the main points of emphasis in Erikson's personality theory?
9. What is meant by epigenetic stages, and what does Erikson call the outcome of each stage?
10. What do you remember of the individual stages of development, and which stage does Erikson view as most important?
11. Which of the concepts of Fromm and Erikson do you see as useful for counseling practice?

REFERENCES

Erikson, E. H. (1965). *The challenge of youth.* Garden City, NY: Anchor Books.
Erikson, E. H. (1950). *Childhood and society.* New York: Norton.
Erikson, E. H. (1974). *Dimensions of a new identity.* New York: Norton.
Erikson, E. H. (1968). *Identity: Youth and crisis.* New York: Norton.
Erikson, E. H. (1964). *Insight and responsibility.* New York: Norton.

Evans, R. I. (1966). *Dialogue with Erich Fromm.* New York: Harper & Row.
Evans, R. I. (1967). *Dialogue with Erik Erikson.* New York: Dutton.
Fromm, E. (1962). *The art of loving.* New York: Harper & Row.
Fromm, E. (1969). *Escape from freedom.* New York: Holt, Rinehart & Winston.
Fromm, E. (1947). *Man for himself.* Greenwich, CT: Fawcett.
Fromm, E. (1950). *Psychoanalysis and religion.* New Haven, CT: Yale University Press.
Fromm, E. (1955). *The sane society.* Greenwich, CT: Fawcett.
Fromm, E. (1966). *Socialist humanism.* Garden City, NJ: Doubleday.
Woodward, K. L. (1994, May 23). An identity of wisdom. *Newsweek,* p. 56.

CHAPTER 7

LEARNING THEORY OF DOLLARD AND MILLER

TO UNDERSTAND Dollard and Miller's theory, we need to briefly explore the premises of behaviorism, on which their theory is built. Behaviorism is usually defined as a school of thought that recognizes observable behavior of "living organisms" as the only appropriate object of psychological concerns. All human behavior occurs according to laws, many of which have been identified. Human behavior can be learned and unlearned since it is the product of objective determinants. Behaviorism professes to be scientific and deterministic in nature: since "free" human reactions to stimuli are weak and infrequent, "determinism [is] a fruitful working hypothesis" (Logan, 1959, p. 295).

Personality has no real existence, in the behavioral perspective, and is not regarded as the **source** of human behavior. It is merely an **inference** derived from overt, observable, and measurable behavior. Behaviorism emphasizes empirical research, which it equates with therapy: "Research is treatment and treatment is research" (Thoresen & Coates, 1980, p. 10). Since behaviorism offers a systematized technology for producing relatively rapid behavior changes, it is widely used in education and counseling.

THREE MAJOR FIGURES IN BEHAVIORISM

Ivan Pavlov (1849–1936)

Pavlov was a Russian physiologist who rejected the traditional idealist assumption of the existence of spirit (or soul) and turned to materialism as his philosophy. All mental phenomena had to be interpreted as resulting from material processes. By throwing the gauntlet "in the face of tradition," Pavlov became the protagonist of an ideological framework prevalent in behaviorist thinking (Wells, 1956).

His theory of **classical conditioning** is based on the linkage of two stimuli. One elicits a response by its very nature and is called **unconditioned stimulus** — S_u; for instance, meat paste that Pavlov presented to a hungry dog would produce salivation. The other stimulus is neutral in itself. Presenting it, however, along with the unconditioned stimulus makes it acquire stimulus power through close linkage with the S_u. It is called **conditioned stimulus** — S_c. In Pavlov's experiment the sound of a bell (S_c) was repeatedly linked with the presentation of meat (S_u). Eventually, the dog would salivate as a response to the ringing of the bell even when no meat paste was presented. This latter response was no longer an **unconditioned response** (R_u) of the dog's organism but a **conditioned response** (R_c). To maintain its efficacy, however, a conditioned stimulus needs to be adequately reinforced by presenting it jointly with the unconditioned stimulus (see Fig. 8).

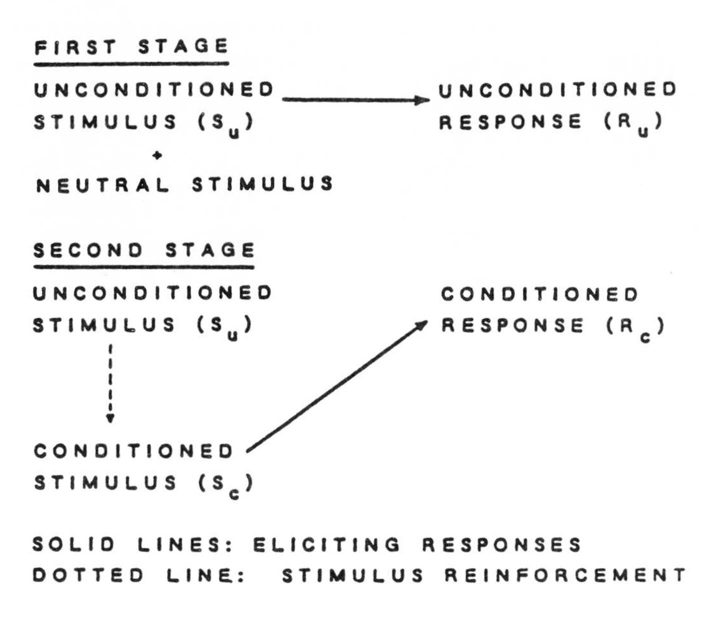

Figure 8. Diagram of Pavlov's classical conditioning.

Clark L. Hull (1884-1952)

Hull developed the fundamentals of learning theory that were later used by Dollard and Miller. He became interested in Pavlov's research on conditioned reflexes of animals. He concurred with Pavlov's focus on the prevalent role of stimuli but differed from Pavlovian theory by relating the S–R sequence to human behavior. He also differed from Pavlov by his explanation of how stimuli influence the organism. In his view the impact of stimuli lies in initiating processes for the reduction of innate organismic drives. Hull perceived learning to be the outcome of **drive reduction** processes.

Learning is effective because of the satisfaction the organism derives from drive reduction. This explains why anticipatory responses are produced by the organism even prior to the completion of the process. The linkage of stimulus, response, and reward generates a number of **habits** in the behavior of individuals. Hull's research extended also to the **delay of reinforcement** in the learning process and to the analysis of behavior as a chain of smaller S–R elements (Hilgard & Marquis, 1961).

B.F. Skinner (1904–1990)

Skinner is the originator of the **operant conditioning** theory built on Thorndike's instrumental conditioning. He postulated that an organism emits spontaneous behaviors not elicited by identifiable stimuli. Such behaviors are called **operants.** The key concept in Skinner's theory is **reinforcement.** Positive reinforcement is a reward; negative reinforcement is the removal of an aversive stimulus. When an operant is reinforced, the likelihood of the recurrence of the behavior increases. The reinforcer assumes the role of stimulus; the reinforced behavior parallels a **conditioned response.**

Skinner developed a number of reinforcement schedules contingent on time intervals—fixed and variable interval reinforcement—or based on the number of responses—ratio reinforcement (fixed and variable ratio). Another strategy developed by Skinner is called **successive approximation.** Behavior is gradually shaped by reinforcing steps that the individual takes toward the envisioned target behavior (Skinner, 1953).

The essential differences between Pavlov's and Skinner's theories of conditioning can be stated in these terms: (1) To avoid extinction of a conditioned response, Pavlov's classical conditioning uses **stimulus reinforcement,** an occasional linkage of the conditioned stimulus with the unconditioned stimulus. (2) To avoid extinction of a conditioned response, Skinner's operant conditioning **reinforces the response,** using one of the reinforcement schedules.

BIOGRAPHICAL DATA ON JOHN DOLLARD (1900-1980) AND NEAL E. MILLER (B. 1909)

Both men were born in Wisconsin: Dollard in Menasha, Miller in Milwaukee. Dollard obtained his doctoral degree in sociology from the University of Chicago and in 1931–32 went to Germany as a research fellow in social psychology to study at the Berlin Psychoanalytic Institute. After his return, he accepted a professorship at Yale University, where he stayed throughout his entire professional career. He held academic appointments in anthropology, sociology, and psychology—a clear indication of his interdisciplinary interests. During World War II, Dollard served as consultant to the Secretary of War and did research on soldier behavior under the stress of battle. He retired from his teaching post in 1969 as professor emeritus.

Neal Miller earned his doctorate in psychology at Yale University. During his graduate studies he was associated with Hull and Dollard, both of whom significantly influenced his professional career. After graduation he went to Europe, under the auspices of the Social Science Research Council, and underwent psychoanalytic training in Vienna. He spent a major part of his teaching and research career at Yale and later joined the staff of Rockefeller University.

Dollard and Miller published three major books, in which they discussed their research findings and formulated their theory: *Frustration and aggression* in 1939 (with associates), *Social learning and imitation* in 1941, and *Personality and psychotherapy* in 1950.

MAIN EMPHASIS OF THE LEARNING THEORY

Although their intellectual orientation was rooted in behaviorism, Dollard and Miller decided to obtain psychoanalytic training and thus participated in two opposite worlds of scientific ideology. Only if we are aware of this dual orientation of the theorists can we fully understand and appreciate the nature of their theory: it is an **integration of psychoanalysis and behaviorism** in the context of a given sociocultural environment. "The ultimate goal is to combine the vitality of psychoanalysis, the rigor of the natural-science laboratory, and the facts of culture" (Dollard & Miller, 1950, p. 3).

The central theme of Dollard and Miller is the learning process, based on the stimulus-response sequence which they use for explaining major concepts in personality functioning, such as (1) intrapsychic processes, (2) the nature and development of personality, (3) the unconscious, and (4) the origins of neuroses.

THE LEARNING PROCESS

Dollard and Miller formulated their concept of the learning process and identified its components in clear, simple terms:

> The learner must be driven to make the response and rewarded for having responded in the presence of the cue. This may be expressed in a homely way by saying that in order to learn one must want something, notice something, do something, and get something. Stated more exactly, these factors are drive, cue, response, and reinforcement. (Miller & Dollard, 1941, p. 2.)

The diagram of this sequence can be found in Figure 9; its components will be explained individually.

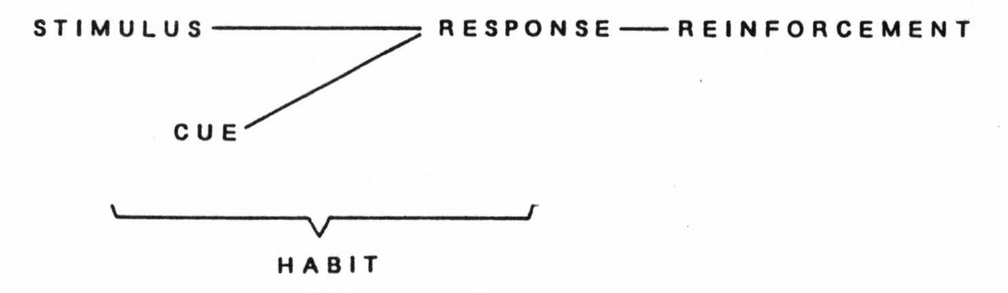

Figure 9. Diagram of Dollard and Miller's learning sequence.

Drive

A drive is any strong stimulus that elicits a response. It is also called **motivation.** Anything that can motivate fits the category of drive. Some drives are **external events,** e.g., an electric shock, or irritating, loud music, etc. Others are innate and are called **primary drives,** such as pain, hunger, thirst, bitter cold, or sexual urge. On the basis of primary drives, the individual learns secondary drives that will be discussed later in this chapter.

Cue

Whereas a drive impels the individual to act, "cues determine when he will respond, where he will respond, and which response he will make" (Miller & Dollard, 1941, p. 21). The cue is also a motivator but its impelling force is more specific. Each cue is distinct in the way it **modifies** the driving power of a stimulus. For instance, hunger pangs motivate a person to eat something; the marquee of a restaurant or the sign of a fast-food store may help the person decide how to respond to the stimulus: by having a full meal or getting a quick snack. It follows that drives and cues have a close functional relationship. A drive that requires a fairly specific response is said to have cue value; on the other hand, a cue may reflect the strength and assume the role of the stimulus, compelling to action by itself.

Response

A response is caused by the motivational force of a drive and by the directional influence of a cue. It is important that some response be elicited for the learning process to take place. Learning cannot occur unless a response is reinforced. In the view of Dollard and Miller, the success of education and therapy largely depends on the ability of professionals to have the learners or patients make appropriate responses that would provide opportunities for reinforcement.

It should be added that certain intrapersonal, covert responses may trigger a series of internal events. Dollard and Miller offer the example of fear elicited by an external drive. The fear, initially a response, assumes the capacity of a cue and elicits one or more internal responses before an overt response of the organism is made.

Reinforcement

Reinforcement is any event "that strengthens the tendency for a response to be repeated" (Dollard & Miller, 1950, p. 39). In concrete terms, reinforcement equals **drive reduction**. The drives may be intrapersonal (hunger pangs, sex urges) or may come from external sources (glare of the sun, loud or shrill sounds). In either case "a prompt reduction in the strength of the drive acts as a reinforcement" (Dollard & Miller, 1950, p. 40). A good meal will reduce the drive of hunger, and moving one's chair to a shady spot will reduce the unpleasant glare. The probability that such reinforced responses will be repeated has increased.

PERSONALITY: ITS NATURE AND DEVELOPMENT

Dollard and Miller call the stimulus/cue-response sequence a **habit,** a concept developed and frequently used by Hull. Personal habits are learned through reinforcement; because of such acquired habits, a person responds to certain cues more readily than to others.

In the view of Dollard and Miller, **personality** is not innate but has been **acquired in childhood** through the learning process. It **consists of habits** that characterize a person's behavior.

From Primary to Secondary Drives

As earlier mentioned, a person is born with **innate** or **primary drives,** e.g., pain, hunger, and thirst. These drives help maintain the person's physiological life, beginning with the first days of infancy. Personality development is perceived by Dollard and Miller in terms of acquiring a repertoire of **secondary drives.** These are seen as elaborations of primary drives in the sociocultural context of one's environment. They "serve as a facade behind which the functions of the underlying innate drives are hidden" (Dollard & Miller, 1950, p. 32).

The actual learning process happens as follows: A previously neutral cue, when sufficiently often paired with a primary drive, acquires the capacity to elicit responses and thus becomes a secondary drive. For instance, the type of food offered to a hungry person will affect the person's taste. Instead of being hungry in general terms, an Italian is probably hungry for pasta, a Hungarian for goulash, and an American for steak or a hamburger. Secondary drives can be viewed as providing maintenance of human life in the context of a given society or culture.

Educational Applications

In the developmental process of personality, the first six years are crucial. Along with secondary drives, the child acquires the knowledge of **secondary reinforcements,** e.g., a smile of mother, a thank-you note, money to buy candy, etc. Dollard and Miller recommend that parents maintain a supportive attitude in dealing with the child, particularly in the first two years of the child's life. They consider four training situations to be of major importance: (1) the feeding situation, (2) the cleanliness training situation, (3) early sex training, and (4) training to control anger.

NEUROSES: UNCONSCIOUS CONFLICTS

Dollard and Miller used their learning approach to explain major Freudian concepts, particularly the unconscious and neuroses.

The Unconscious

In their view, the unconscious consists of drives, cues, and responses that occurred without being understood or labeled: "Since the effective use of speech develops gradually and may not be established for certain categories until long after the child has learned to say 'mama,' the period during which major parts of social learning are unconscious extends over a considerable number of years and has no set boundaries" (Dollard & Miller, 1950, p. 198).

Dollard and Miller point out that the unconscious is not limited to childhood. Even adults may have difficulties in labeling their behavior or its factors. For instance, neurotics are **unable to describe** their own conflicts.

From Childhood Conflicts to Adulthood Neuroses

The unconscious is closely related to the formation of neuroses, which are considered by Dollard and Miller (1950) to be **unconscious conflicts learned in infancy and early childhood:**

> Young children can be subject to more extreme conditions than adults endure, except perhaps when adults are exposed to combat situations in time of war. . . .
>
> It is not surprising, then, that acute emotional conflicts occur in childhood. The infant has not learned to wait, not knowing the world's inescapable routines; to hope, and thus to assure itself that the good moment will return and that the evil occasion will pass; to reason and plan, and thus to escape present disorder by constructing the future in a controlled way. (p. 130.)

According to Dollard and Miller, neuroses are taught by parents. Some may offer their children little emotional support or stimulation to speak and think. Others present threatening cues on sexual matters; they may teach children the names of all parts of the body except for the sex organs or may punish their children if they explore their genital area (Dollard, 1942).

Children typically experience sex-related approach—avoidance conflicts; approach stands for any sexual initiative, avoidance refers to the fear of punishment. Parenthetically, two other types of conflict should be mentioned: the approach-approach conflict and the avoidance-avoidance conflict. The former involves two positive alternatives, e.g., being torn between equally desirable goals; the latter involves two negative alternatives, e.g., having to choose one type of punishment over another.

Unconscious conflicts learned in childhood generate anxiety and stimulate the emergence of neuroses in adult life. Fortunately, since neuroses have been learned, they can also be unlearned, even after many years of psychological pain.

APPLICATIONS TO COUNSELING

Behavioral theory in general and Dollard and Miller's learning theory in particular offer a number of operational concepts and strategies that can be used in counseling practice. Among them are:

1. Skinner's strategy of behavior modification, particularly through the process of successive approximation
2. Dollard and Miller's learning sequence consisting of drive/cue, response, and reinforcement through drive reduction
3. Their view of personality development by means of learning secondary drives
4. Their concept of the unconscious and the importance of language for mitigating its power
5. The nature and development of neuroses

CHAPTER REVIEW

1. What is meant by behaviorism as a psychological school of thought?
2. What is the basis of classical conditioning?
3. What is the main principle of operant conditioning, and how does it differ from classical conditioning?
4. How did Hull perceive his S–R learning process, particularly the reinforcement?

5. Do you recall some autobiographical data on Dollard and Miller?
6. What is the main emphasis of the learning theory?
7. Can you describe the components of Dollard and Miller's learning sequence?
8. Why is the response to a drive needed if learning is to occur?
9. How did Dollard and Miller perceive the nature of personality?
10. What is meant by primary and secondary drives, and how are secondary drives learned?
11. How does learning theory explain the unconscious?
12. What is the nature of neuroses, and how do they originate?
13. Which concepts of behaviorism and learning theory in particular do you find useful for counseling practice?

REFERENCES

Dollard, J. (1942). *Victory over fear.* New York: Reynal & Hitchcock.

Dollard, J., & Miller, N. E. (1950). *Personality and psychotherapy: An analysis in terms of learning, thinking, and culture.* New York: McGraw-Hill.

Dollard, J., Miller, N. E., Doob, L. W., Mowrer, O. H. & Sears, R. R. (1939). *Frustration and aggression.* New Haven, CT: Yale University Press.

Hilgard, E. R., & Marquis, D. G. (1961). *Conditioning and learning* (rev. ed. by G. A. Kimble). New York: Appleton-Century.

Logan, F. A. (1959). The Hull-Spence approach. In S. Koch (Ed.): *Psychology: A study of science* (Vol. 2, pp. 293–358). New York: McGraw-Hill.

Miller, N. E., & Dollard, J. (1941). *Social learning and imitation.* New Haven, CT: Yale University Press.

Skinner, B. F. (1953). *Science and human behavior.* New York: Macmillan.

Thoresen, C. E., & Coates, T. J. (1980). What does it mean to be a behavioral therapist? In C. E. Thoresen (Ed.): *The behavior therapist* (pp. 1–41). Monterey, CA: Brooks-Cole.

Wells, H. K. (1956). *Ivan P. Pavlov: Toward a scientific psychology and psychiatry.* New York: International Publishers.

CHAPTER 8

TRAIT AND FACTOR THEORY

RAYMOND B. CATTELL (B. 1905)

THE THEORY presented in this chapter is known for its effort to explore personality by describing and analyzing attributes of human behavior. Since ancient times, scientists have been eager to identify behaviors that set individuals apart from each other and to establish a taxonomy of personality types. For instance, Hippocrates (460–360 B.C.) differentiated four personality types: (1) the **sanguinic** type, an optimistic, energetic person; (2) the **choleric** type, an irascible person; (3) the **melancholic** type, a person prone to depression; and (4) the **phlegmatic** type, an apathetic person who shows minimal emotional reactions. In more recent times, Jung developed his own typology, using two basic types of introversion and extraversion, paired with four faculties or functions: thinking, feeling, sensation, and intuition.

The strength of Cattell's approach is its proven ability to offer an empirically documented analysis of personality components. This has been accomplished by a statistical procedure known as **factor analysis.** Ironically, Cattell's statistical emphasis is also the reason why he is criticized. Although his methodology has provided valuable prerequisites for the construction of personality inventories, it has not done justice to the interpretation of many dynamic processes in human life.

Cattell (1959) downplays the role of clinical (and naturalistic) observation: "The clinician has his heart in the right place, but perhaps we may say that he remains a little fuzzy in his head" (p. 45). He prefers to assess personality on the basis of indirect information obtained through psychological tests and rating instruments.

BIOGRAPHICAL DATA ON RAYMOND CATTELL

Born in Staffordshire, England, Cattell received his entire education from primary grades to university studies in British schools. He earned his doctorate in psychology at the University of London. After eight years of professional work as university lecturer and practicing psychologist in Britain, Cattell emigrated to the United States.

He lectured at Harvard and Duke universities and in 1944 transferred to the University of Illinois, where he spent two decades of his life. He then moved to Colorado and founded the Institute for Research and Self-Realization in Boulder. Cattell was a prolific writer and constructed several important psychological test instruments, of which the Sixteen Personality Factor Questionnaire (16 PF) is probably the best-known.

POINTS OF EMPHASIS IN CATTELL'S THEORY

1. Cattell used a **descriptive** approach to personality. He believed that unless we can describe a personality well enough so that others can recognize it, our attempt at exploring it would be futile. Basic elements that make the description of personality possible are **traits**, i.e., characteristics inferred from observable behavior typical of a person.

2. Cattell also favored a **predictive** emphasis. Although he believed that "a reasonably complete definition of personality is out of the question," for the purpose of his research he nevertheless offered a "denotative" definition: "Personality is that which permits a prediction of what a person will do in a given situation" (Cattell, 1950, p. 2).

3. Closely linked with his descriptive emphasis is the **psychometric** approach to personality research. In his view, "exact measurement" offers the only firm basis for scientific advances. Psychological testing is one of the means for collecting accurate and quantifiable data for the description of personality. Cattell's theory primarily benefits psychometrists, researchers, and counselors who are test-oriented.

TRAITS AND FACTORS

Trait and **factor** are two basic concepts that need to be explained if we are to fully understand Cattell's theory. The nature of personality, interpretation of behavior, and individual assessment are elaborations and applications of the trait and factor framework. What follows is a succinct classification of traits and a conceptual explanation of factors.

Classification of Traits

Unique and common traits. Most people interpret the term "trait" as a behavioral attribute of a person. Such attributes are inferred from behaviors, which seem to occur with a degree of regularity and consistency. These are **unique traits** as they actually exist in individuals; they are not merely abstract concepts.

For research purposes, Cattell (1946) viewed traits from a different perspective, as "abstractions from concrete, 'operational' behavior" (p. 88). These generalized concepts can be used for describing elements of behavior found in a large number of persons. They are called **common traits.** In Cattell's view, every trait, unique and common, is a collection of responses bound by a certain unity that offers the trait its distinct identity.

Surface and source traits. Cattell (1950) differentiated surface traits and source traits. The former are discovered through observation of overt behavior; the latter are sources or causes of observable behavior attributes.

Constitutional and environmental-mold traits. Constitutional traits have been acquired through heredity; environmental-mold traits have been shaped by environmental influences.

Ability and temperament traits. Ability traits indicate how capable a person is to move toward chosen goals. Cattell has never tired in proposing additional subdivisions. For instance, ability includes intelligence and manual dexterity, and both of these trait-elements are split into still more specific elements.

Temperament traits comprise the innate "tools" of personality, such as sensitivity, impulsiveness, spontaneity, responsiveness, etc.

Dynamic traits are motivational forces that stimulate the organism to action. As will be explained later in this chapter, dynamic traits can be physiological or environmental in nature.

Factors

Traits can be subdivided into trait-elements that were mentioned earlier. These trait-elements are source traits or **factors.** By means of factor analysis, Cattell identified a number of factors and their mutual relationships. As elements of a broader pattern, factors can be defined as **source traits with an attached numerical value,** which expresses their correlation with other factors. Cattell (1950) offers an example of **factor**

loading (assigning them a numerical value): If general intelligence is split into factors, we discover that "the ability in mathematics is loaded about 0.8 or 0.9 with the general factor [intelligence], whereas ability in drawing is loaded only about 0.3 or 0.4" (p. 24). This means that a person of a particular intelligence level will do much better in math than in drawing (0.8 or 0.9 is close to 1.0; 0.3 or 0.4 is farther).

MEANS OF COLLECTING DATA

As a prerequisite for success of the factor-analytical processes, Cattell (1957) had to obtain a large number of surface variables—the raw material for his research—that would involve all conceivable situations "to which humans react." He called this exhaustive collection of behavior patterns **personality sphere** and used three sources of information for describing it:

1. **Life record (L-data).** It is a person's record of behavior in society, such as school records, court records, marriage and divorce records, etc. Such data are obtained from sources other than the subject under study.
2. **Questionnaire (Q-data).** This information is obtained through a self-rating questionnaire administered to the subject and contains his or her self-evaluation. Q-data can then be compared with the external record yielded by L-data to assess the consistency of the findings.
3. **Objective test (T-data).** Such data are provided as the result of objective tests. Various life situations are created in which the person's behavior is scored. It is important that subjects take a test without being aware of the relationship of their responses to test variables that are being scored.

Cattell found that similar factor structures emerged from L-data and Q-data and considered them well-established in human behavior. Personality factors taken from the 16 PF test include: intelligence, ego strength, dominance-submissiveness, emotional sensitivity-hard realism, tension-relaxation, etc.

THE PREDICTIVE NATURE OF PERSONALITY

Cattell's definition of personality as a means for predicting future behavior of a person was presented earlier in this chapter. A definition given by Cattell (1946) elsewhere restates his view in shorter form: "It is that which predicts behavior, given the situation" (p. 566). This definition implies two components of behavior: (1) **traits** of the individual and (2) environmental influences—**situational indices.** Any current behavior of a person can be mathematically expressed in terms of situational indices (s_1, s_2, etc.) and traits (T_1, T_2, etc.) as follows: Behavioral response $= s_1T_1 + s_2T_2 + s_3T_3. \ldots + s_nT_n$.

We can draw two conclusions from Cattell's comments on personality:

1. In accordance with the behaviorist frame of reference, Cattell considers personality an inference of behavior.

2. Although primarily concerned with traits and factors as future determinants of behavior, he does not exclude the impact of environmental influences.

It needs to be added that Cattell (1950) set limits to the predictive ability of his theory: "Whatever degree of theoretical determinism we are prepared to admit in regard to human behavior, it is certain that in practice, no matter how good our measuring instruments and our understanding of the process at work, the accuracy of our predictions is limited" (p. 662).

PERSONALITY DYNAMICS

Cattell (1957) interpreted intrapersonal processes in terms of dynamic traits mentioned earlier. He classified these traits as constitutional (physiological) dynamic traits, which he called ergs, and environmental dynamic traits, which he perceived as sentiments or attitudes.

Ergs as constitutional (physiological) dynamic traits are parallel to primary drives or instincts proposed in other personality theories. Examples of ergs are mating, gregariousness, parental protectiveness, self-assertion, narcissistic sex (self-indulgence), etc.

Sentiments and attitudes are environmental dynamic traits that are similar to emotional and social needs proposed in other personality theories. The difference between sentiments and attitudes lies in their primary functions and relative depth. **Sentiments** are **intrapersonal,** closely related to issues that seem important to a person. They parallel the concept of values and may focus on one's occupation, marriage, religion, homeland, sports, etc.

Most important among them is the **sentiment of self;** it involves self-awareness, self-evaluation, desire for self-control, preservation of one's reputation, discharge of ethical obligations, increase of salary, etc.

Attitudes are **overt expressions** of sentiments and ergs. Cattell (1957) considered them tendencies "to act in a particular way to a situation.... Occasionally the student is troubled by the suspicion that the popular use of 'attitude' does not imply action" (p. 443). Cattell argued that without overt action, at least verbal action, attitudes could not even be inferred.

Process of Subsidiation

In Cattell's view, the dynamic traits are constantly interacting with each other, and the channels of interaction among them form the **dynamic lattice**, which Cattell graphically depicts as a network of passages from ergs to sentiments and on to attitudes. The dynamic interplay, in which attitudes are subsidiary to sentiments and sentiments are subsidiary to ergs is called **subsidiation.**

The following example has been gleaned from a fragment of the dynamic lattice presented by Cattell (1950). In this instance, an individual's attitudes toward a new film, toward divorce reform legislation, and toward the president of the United States express (are subsidiary to) his or her sentiment toward the country. That sentiment, in turn, expresses (is subsidiary to) the ergs of protection, self-assertion, security, and disgust. A simplified diagram of this subsidiation sequence can be found in Figure 10.

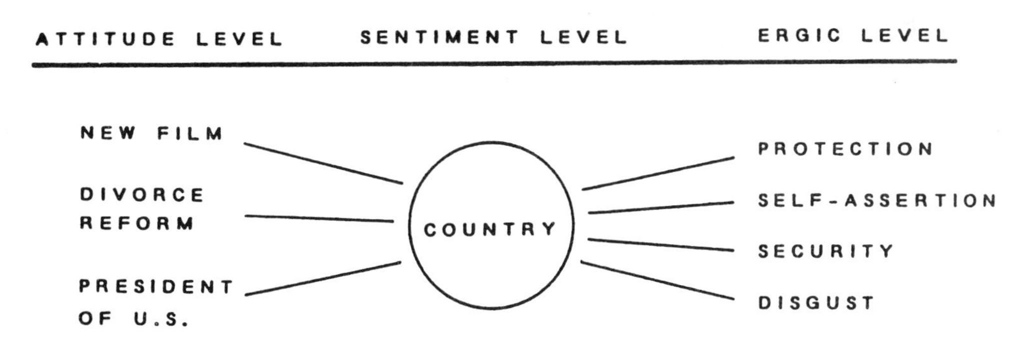

Figure 10. An example of Cattell's subsidiation process.

Intrapersonal Conflicts

Cattell explains all intrapersonal processes in terms of dynamic traits interacting with each other. This applies also to intrapersonal conflicts.

He lists ergs and sentiments and attaches to each a positive or negative value. For instance, a doctoral student who is torn between starting a family and completing her dissertation may have, among others, the following dynamic trait levels: +0.5 husband (sentiment), −0.6 graduate study (sentiment), +0.5 mating (erg), −0.4 fear (erg), +0.3 self-sentiment. Cattell's approach to assessing the strength of the conflict consists of computing the positive and negative weights (numerical values) of the traits and establishing the ratio of conflict on the basis of a mathematical formula.

CATTELL'S CONTRIBUTION TO LEARNING THEORY

The trait profile of a person develops through learning, and Cattell recognized the two major learning processes: classical conditioning and operant conditioning. He added his own kind, **integration learning,** in which "behavior contributes harmoniously to a single life goal or consistent set of goals" (Cattell, 1950, p. 268). This can be accomplished by expressing some ergs while repressing or rechanneling other ergs to generate a long-term internal reinforcement. The process is influenced by the sentiments of self and of the superego.

PERSONALITY DEVELOPMENT

Cattell (1979) viewed personality development to be the result of learning and maturation influenced by the environment. The **child** acquires the sentiments of ego and superego between the ages of two and five. From then on the child endeavors to increase ego strength and extends his or her interests beyond the family. **Adolescence** is a turbulent period, in which the youth seeks independence and works toward integration of his or her personality.

During **maturity** the individual becomes more stable and moves from adolescent planning to selecting realistic goals. Maturity is for Cattell the longest (from 25 to 55 years) and the least eventful period of life. Intelligence, which has reached its peak around age twenty, declines. Cattell (1950) saw, however, the decline as occurring primarily in the area of a person's adaptability rather than previously acquired skills.

Cattell's (1950) view of **old age** was less than optimistic. As the old person's powers weaken, a symbiosis of kindness and aggressiveness emerges in his or her life: "The increasing considerateness brought by age and experience probably produces greater benevolence even though offset by impulsive irritability" (p. 618). Cattell ascribed mental instability and other problems in aging to the rapidly declining health of old people.

APPLICATIONS TO COUNSELING

In spite of the strong research orientation of Cattell, his theory offers certain ideas that may prove useful to counseling practitioners, particularly if they are test-oriented:

1. The concept of trait as behavioral variable
2. Cattell's three ways of collecting information on clients: the life record; the questionnaire; and psychological tests
3. Analysis of individual behavior in terms of its causes—source traits
4. The concept of integration learning

CHAPTER REVIEW

1. What do you remember about Cattell's life?
2. What are his recognized achievements, and what is the criticism of his work?
3. What are the three points of emphasis in Cattell's theory?
4. Can you define traits and classify them?
5. What is meant by a factor?
6. What means of collecting information on individual behavior did Cattell recommend?
7. What is Cattell's definition of personality?
8. How did Cattell explain intrapersonal processes in terms of interaction among dynamic traits?
9. What contribution did Cattell make to learning theory?
10. How did Cattell perceive human development through the life span?
11. Which of Cattell's ideas do you perceive to be useful for counseling practice?

REFERENCES

Cattell, R. B. (1946). *Description and measurement of personality.* Yonkers, NY: World Book.

Cattell, R. B. (1959). Foundations of personality measurement theory in multivari-

ate expression. In B. M. Bass, & I. A. Berg (Eds.): *Objective approaches to personality assessment* (pp. 42–65). Princeton, NJ: Van Nostrand.
Cattell, R. B. (1950). *Personality: A systematic and factual study.* New York: McGraw-Hill.
Cattell, R. B. (1979). *Personality and learning theory.* New York: Springer.
Cattell, R. B. (1957). *Personality and motivation structure and measurement.* Yonkers, NY: World Book.

CHAPTER 9

FIELD THEORY

KURT LEWIN (1890–1947)

LEWIN'S theory presents personality as a dynamic system operating within a field. Lewin draws a map of the individual's life space and graphically portrays the forces that operate within that space. Allport (1947) considered him one of the most original psychologists of the century. It is a paradox that although Lewin formulated his theory to interpret primarily individual behavior, he has been most influential in the area of group dynamics.

LEWIN'S LIFE

Lewin was born in a small town in eastern Germany (today's Poland), where his father owned a general store. The family moved to Berlin when Kurt was still a teenager. After high school and relatively short soujourns at the universities of Freiburg and Munich, Lewin enrolled at the University of Berlin and received his doctorate in psychology there.

Having served in the army during World War I, Lewin began his academic career at the University of Berlin. There he associated with two proponents of Gestalt psychology, Wolfgang Koehler and Max Wertheimer, many of whose ideas he later incorporated into his theoretical framework.

In 1932, Lewin came to the United States as a visiting professor at Stanford and made the move permanent the following year. He taught for two years at Cornell University but devoted the largest part of his professional career in this country (ten years) to teaching and research at the State University of Iowa. Eventually, he accepted a position as director of the Research Center for Group Dynamics at the Massachusetts Institute of Technology, where he applied his field theory to structured group work and social situations in general. He attracted a large following of devoted students. His untimely death of a heart infarct in 1947 abruptly ended his work after only two years of tenure.

POINTS OF EMPHASIS IN LEWIN'S THEORY

1. Lewin's theory is **topological** in nature. This means that all his concepts have found a spatial expression. He considered topology to "be based on the relationship between 'part' and 'whole' or in other words on the concepts of 'being included in' " (Lewin, 1936, p. 87). This lends his theory a degree of concreteness and facilitates its understanding.

2. Lewin emphasized that topological concepts were in fact, **mathematical.** For instance, the concepts of force, distance, and direction could be best expressed in mathematical terms by the use of formulas. Lewin (1935) did not believe, however, that statistics could fully interpret the dynamics of personality and "the actual total situation in its concrete individuality" (p. 68).

3. By means of topological dimensions and features of the life space, Lewin was able to interpret intrapersonal dynamics and the interdependence of the **person and the environment.** Furthermore, intrapersonal and environmental processes were shown as being closely linked.

4. Lewin extensively used **differentiation,** a process adopted from Gestalt psychology, to explain the development of personality. By differentiation, he meant **breaking up a whole** phenomenon **into parts.** For instance, when we visit a city the first time, we perceive it in its totality. It is only after we have become acquainted with the various sections of the city and its suburbs that we can form a **differentiated concept** which is more detailed and accurate. Differentiation is closely linked with cognitive processes.

STRUCTURE OF PERSONALITY

Lewin's use of drawings was not primarily for didactic purposes but rather was employed to facilitate mathematical interpretations. A circle designates the person (P), which is surrounded by an elliptic field—the psychological environment (E). The person and the psychological environment form together the life space (L), outside of which is the foreign hull.

Lewin (1936) expressed this basic personality structure by means of a formula: $L = P + E$. Figure 11 presents the elements of this formula in their topological relationships. The drawing of a real, living personality would also contain differentiations (divisions of the whole into parts) both in the person and in the psychological environment. The personality of a living individual will be discussed and graphically described later in this chapter.

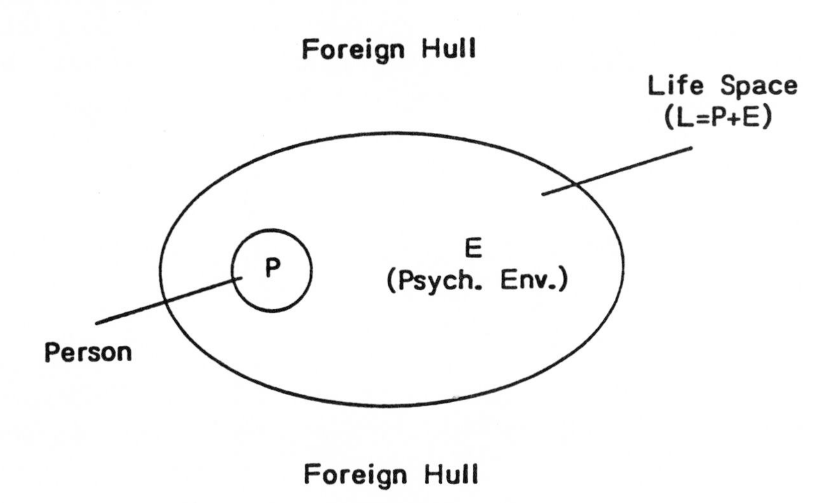

Figure 11. Lewin's topological structure of personality.

Life Space and Foreign Hull

The life space, of which the person is a part, contains **psychological facts** determining the person's current behavior. Lewin considered behavior to be the function of the life space and expressed that functional relationship by his formula $B = f(L)$ that can also be stated as $B = f(P + E)$.

It follows that the life space is Lewin's central concept and coincides with the dimensions of personality. Because of its importance, the life space will be explained more thoroughly later in terms of its two main components—the psychological environment and the person.

The foreign hull that lies beyond the life space has no direct bearing on the person's behavior, since it consists of elements not attended to by the person. Some elements of the foreign hull may, however, eventually impact the person and exert a direct influence on his or her behavior. For instance, the person may not be aware of a new bill discussed in the state legislature on additional taxation; if the bill is passed, however, it will influence his or her behavior because of the added tax burden.

PSYCHOLOGICAL ENVIRONMENT

To communicate with the outside world, the person has to use the psychological environment. This indicates its importance to the person. In fact, the psychological environment could be described as the **total reality accessible to the person** at any given time.

Lewin's (1936) principle of contemporaneity ("In representing the life space therefore we take into account only what is contemporary," p. 35) means that all psychological processes occurring in the life space are **in the present**, including past experiences and plans for the future.

Psychological Regions and Facts

The psychological environment contains **regions**, which are enclosed by boundaries with various degrees of thickness, solidity, and elasticity. The regions themselves can be rigid or fluid. Another quality of the regions is their relative nearness or remoteness from each other. Every region contains a **psychological fact** that may be a person, an object, or an idea, which has some bearing on the person's behavior. Lewin (1935) described the content of regions that are typically found in a child's psychological environment:

> In the environment there are, as we have seen, many objects and events of quasi-physical and quasi-social nature, such as rooms, halls, tables, chairs, a bed, a cap, knife and fork, things that fall down, turn over, can start and go of themselves; there are dogs, friends, grown-ups, neighbors, someone who rarely gets cross, and someone who is always strict and disagreeable. (p. 76.)

Since healthy people have numerous interests, they possess many regions in their psychological environment (see Fig. 12). If, however, an individual is the victim of a traumatic experience (e.g., a serious automobile accident with injuries) a sudden change may occur in the psychological field. Whereas earlier it was divided into perhaps two dozen regions, the accident reduced their number to only three: injury, shock, and expense. As the impact of the accident diminishes, the person experiences additional differentiations (divisions) of the psychological environment, and eventually the usual repertoire of his or her regions and psychological facts returns.

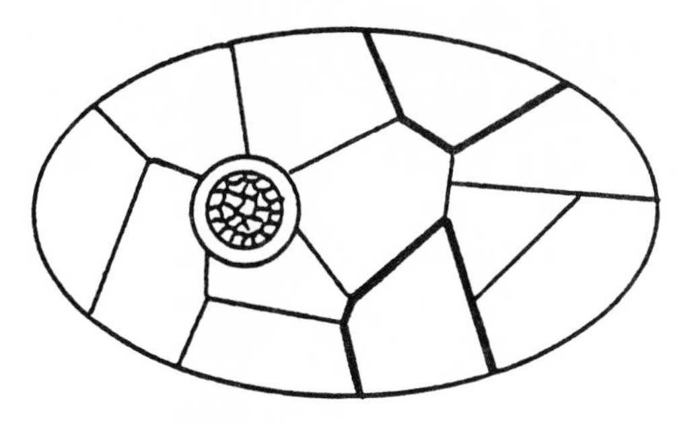

**Boundaries of Regions:
Elastic or Thick**

Figure 12. Life space divided into regions.

Valences

Each psychological fact has a specific value or meaning for the person, which is mathematically expressed as **valence:** "The kind (sign) and strength of the valence of an object or event thus depends directly upon the momentary condition of the needs of the individual concerned; the valences of environmental objects and the needs of the individual are correlative" (Lewin, 1935, p. 78).

Valences should be perceived as indicators of a positive or negative value that, at any given time, the person assigns to individual psychological facts (and their regions) in the environment. Lewin does not use numerical measures to indicate the relative strength of valences, but recognizes that their intensity may range from weak to very strong.

For instance, a person who rarely goes to the movies may have a slight minus valence attached to the psychological fact "movies." The same person will, however, assign a highly positive valence to a particular movie that has been recommended to him or her by a friend because of its outstanding portrayal of the life of Abraham Lincoln. In this instance three regions of the psychological environment have mutually communicated. One region contained the person offering the information; another region contained movies; a third region contained the person's interest in Abraham Lincoln, which made the movie attractive. The communication of two or more regions with each other is called an **event.**

THE PERSON

Boundary Zone and Inner-Personal Region

The person is a differentiated part of the life space—its central part (see Fig. 13). The boundary zone of the person consists of the **perceptual-motor region** or area. Any input from the environment enters the **inner-personal region** through the perceptual-motor area that rings the person. Any initiative or behavioral response of the person leaves the inner-personal region through the same perceptual-motor area. It follows that this ring-like area has a dual function in its role as **communication zone** between the person and the environment.

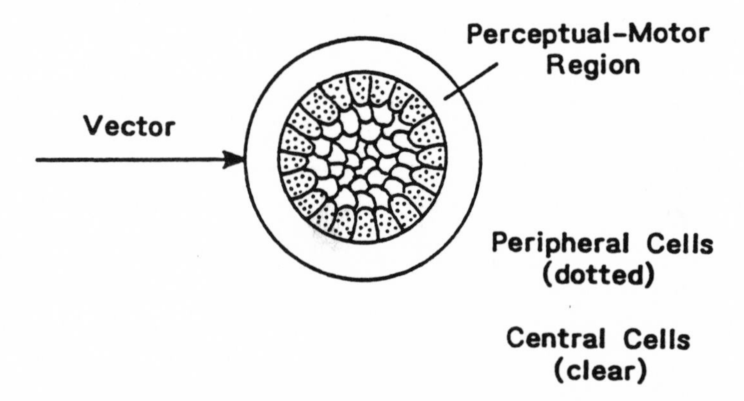

Figure 13. The person divided into regions (enlarged).

Lewin likens this dual function to the operation of the human eye, which can perceive and express feelings with equal ease. In his view, the perceptual-motor region "seems to possess a relatively high unity: it is difficult to carry out four or five unrelated activities at the same time" (Lewin, 1936, p. 179). Therefore, the region is portrayed as solid, not divided into cells.

Cells of the inner-personal region contain **psychological** and **social needs** along with **perceptual** and **communicatory** capacities (seeing, hearing, speech, body language, etc.). There are two kinds of cells, **peripheral** and **central.** The difference between them lies in the degree of intensity and depth associated with the psychological processes that are transacted by them. The peripheral cells are in closer contact with the perceptual-motor region than are the central cells. Therefore, a spontaneous conversation of lesser depth would be handled by peripheral cells since it

> usually occurs more readily when events of more peripheral strata are concerned. One speaks about personal matters only under special circumstances... The way to the peripheral regions of the person is almost always open. But it is difficult to touch the real core of the person. (Lewin, 1936, p. 180)

The arrangement of peripheral and central cells changes according to momentary states of the individual's thinking and feeling, and according to new situations as they emerge. It is well to remember that the entire life space including the person's internal structure is in the process of ongoing change: "An example of a relatively simple change of dynamic relations between the different strata is the transition from a state of superficial anger to a state of profound anger" (Lewin, 1936, p. 181). Similarly, a person who wants to exercise a high degree of self-control in a particular situation shows a greater separation of intrapersonal cells from the perceptual-motor region than when he or she is in a relaxed mood.

DYNAMICS OF THE LIFE SPACE

The life space is filled with psychic energy that permeates equally the person and the environment. Lewin (1935) was ambiguous about the energy's source and suggested that "when the concept of energy is used here, ... the question may be left quite open as to whether or not one should ultimately go back to physical forces" (p. 46). The psychic energy manifests itself primarily in two ways: in the person through tensions and in the environment through vectors.

Dynamics of the Person

The person's internal structure has a tendency toward **equilibrium.** This state of complete balance of energy is, however, frequently interrupted by **tensions.** Any desire a person may have or any physiological need that should be met causes tension within the inner-personal region. The satisfaction of the desire or the satiation of the physiological need removes the tension and restores equilibrium. In the process, the inner-personal cells interact with each other and the tension may be shared, thus producing a multiple response to the original urge. For example, the release of sexual energy may be combined with social fulfillment, or the desire for money may lead to higher motivation at work.

Dynamics of the Psychological Environment

As noted earlier, every region of the environment has a particular meaning for the person, and it is expressed as a positive or negative valence. Positive valences attract while negative valences repel the person. Depending on the momentary state of the person's needs, a psychological fact may greatly increase its attractiveness. This generates a force in the psychological environment, which is represented by a **vector** (see Fig. 13). The vector is a line with an arrow pointing in a given direction. The length of the line indicates the strength or intensity of the force, while the arrow clarifies the direction in which the force moves (Lewin, 1938).

The vector pushes the person in the direction of a psychological fact. At times, more than one vector is involved to help the person pass through the environment and, if need be, circumvent regions that act as barriers. The movement of the person toward the desired goal is called **locomotion.** Locomotion is not always a real event; it can also be imaginary, e.g., mere planning, fantasizing, or even daydreaming. Imaginary locomotion is easier to undertake than one based on reality because the path to be followed is blocked by fewer firm boundaries.

Parenthetically, it may be added that the concept of vector has been turned to practical use by professionals in other fields that interested Lewin (1948). Consultants, managers, and social workers have been using it for planning institutional changes through force field analysis (see Fig. 14).

DEVELOPMENT OF PERSONALITY

Although the field theory does not spell out any time sequence needed for developmental processes, it nevertheless offers an interpretation of personality development. This is accomplished through the processes of **differentiation** and **integration.** As the individual matures, both the person and the environment are being divided into more regions. This process continues until it reaches the optimal level of differentiation appropriate for the individual.

Differentiation promotes a variety of concerns and makes the person's

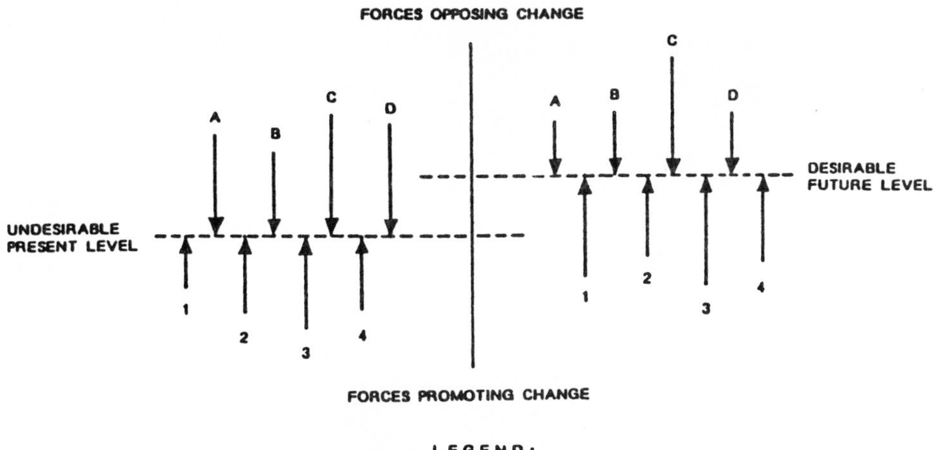

Figure 14. Diagram of force field analysis used in a school (Adapted from V. J. Drapela (1983). *The counselor as consultant and supervisor.* Springfield, IL: Charles C Thomas.)

interests widen. To assure unity of purpose and to make the person self-directive, another process has to set in: "The increasing differentiation of the life space into relatively separated subparts is somehow counteracted by the increasing organization of the life space. There is a wealth of material which indicates this increasing organization with age" (Lewin, 1951, p. 108).

This final step toward full maturity is the process of **integration.** Certain inner-personal cells develop higher levels of tension and thus exercise a functional control over other cells. Briefly stated, integration is a hierarchy of tensions that has been established among the subsystems of the person.

REGRESSION

Lewin (1951) interpreted this psychoanalytic concept according to his own frame of reference. Instead of viewing it exclusively as the turning back of libido to an earlier developmental stage, he perceived it in broader terms: "If one refers to the individual himself instead of his libido one can represent the situation which is said to underlie the turning back of the libido by a simple topological diagram" (Lewin, 1951, p. 91).

Regression occurs when a person endeavors to reach need satisfaction in accordance with his or her level of maturity. This appropriate form of need satisfaction—contained in a region of the psychological environment and identified as G+ (goal)—is, however, hard to reach. Under the circumstances, the person turns to another region in the environment that offers some satisfaction of the need, although at a less mature level (marked as G'). According to Lewin's theory, regression means that one is giving up his or her attempt to overcome a barrier that has emerged and settles for a lesser goal than originally intended.

To graphically illustrate both the progress of personality development or the backward path of regression, Lewin insisted that the various moves be shown by separate drawings of the life space. Since the psychological field always exists in the present, one drawing could not express the time-related dimension of the processes.

APPLICATIONS TO COUNSELING

Lewin's field theory has a number of concepts that may help counselors form a concrete image of the interplay of personality dynamics and enrich the counseling process.

1. The concepts of life space and foreign hull
2. The organization of the psychological environment with its regions, psychological facts, and valences
3. The organization of the person in terms of boundary zone and inner-personal region
4. The interpretation of personality dynamics and the interaction of the person and psychological environment
5. The explanation of personality development through differentiation and integration

CHAPTER REVIEW

1. What do you remember of Lewin's biography?
2. Which are the points of emphasis in the field theory?
3. What is the difference between life space and foreign hull?
4. What can be the content of regions that comprise the psychological environment?
5. What is meant by an event resulting from the communication of regions?

6. What are valences?
7. Into what regions is the person divided?
8. What is the functional difference between peripheral and central cells in the person?
9. What is meant by tension and equilibrium in the inner-personal region?
10. What is meant by vector and locomotion?
11. How did Lewin explain personality development and the process of regression?
12. How can counselors best use the concepts from Lewin's field theory?

REFERENCES

Allport, G. W. (1947). The genius of Kurt Lewin. *Journal of Personality, 16,* 1–10.

Lewin, K. (1935). *A dynamic theory of personality.* New York: McGraw-Hill.

Lewin, K. (1938). *The conceptual representation and the measurement of psychological forces.* Durham, NC: Duke University Press.

Lewin, K. (1951). *Field theory in social science.* Westport, CT: Greenwood Press.

Lewin, K. (1936). *Principles of topological psychology.* New York: McGraw-Hill.

Lewin, K. (1948). *Resolving social conflicts: Selected papers on group dynamics.* New York: Harper.

CHAPTER 10

SYSTEMATIC ECLECTICISM

GORDON W. ALLPORT (1897-1967)

AS A THEORIST, Allport integrated a number of contributions from American and European psychology of the first half of this century and placed them into a new perspective. In America he absorbed elements of the positivistic and statistical orientations; while in Europe he developed an understanding of the unity of the person and a healthy respect for values. His professional legacy combines scientific objectivity with concerns for social issues. An example is his extensive study on prejudice (Allport, 1954).

Although called a trait theorist by many, he rejected or modified some aspects of that approach and did not even object to being labeled an "anti-trait theorist." Above all, Allport was a humanist closely related in friendship to Carl Rogers, Kurt Lewin, and Gardner Murphy, whom he called "first cousins of my thinking" (Evans, 1971).

Allport (1968) proposed an eclectic theory that frequently served as catalyst of heterogeneous or even conflicting ideas. In his view, eclecticism is "a system that seeks the solution of fundamental problems by selecting and uniting what it regards as true in the several specialized approaches to psychological science" (pp. 5–6). Allport was, however, quick to make a distinction of two kinds of eclecticism: (1) **jackdaw eclecticism** that indiscriminately gathers unrelated ideas and (2) **systematic eclecticism** that attempts to form a united, integrated structure out of various contributions by others.

To different degrees, Allport was influenced by Gestalt psychology, psychoanalysis, Lewin's field theory, trait theory, and behaviorism. His own theoretical structure absorbed at least certain aspects of most of these approaches. He believed that this combination of ideas had merit since:

> American psychology itself is a sort of eclectic edifice. Virtually all leading concepts are borrowed from Europe. . . . To these we have added the starch of

> stiffer method, a draft of our own pragmatism, and a dash of optimism. We have even engaged in conceptual cohabitation, by joining psychoanalysis with stimulus-response as well as with the culture concept. (Allport, 1968, pp. 14–15.)

ALLPORT'S LIFE

Allport was born in Montezuma, Indiana, in 1897, as the family's youngest child and was delivered by his own father, a country physician. Shortly after his birth, the family moved to Cleveland, where young Gordon received his elementary and high school education. Both of his parents emphasized the value of education and were role models of strong religious and ethical convictions. Allport did his undergraduate work at Harvard, earning a bachelor's degree in economics and philosophy. He then applied for an instructorship at Robert College in Istanbul and spent a year in that city where East meets West. On his way home he stopped in Vienna and visited Freud; the visit was, however, less than satisfying and did not influence him in the direction of psychoanalytic training.

Allport returned to Harvard and completed there his doctoral work in psychology in record time and yet allowed sufficient time and energy to romance, which eventually led to marriage. At the age of twenty-four he defended his dissertation that dealt explicitly with personality. For the next two years he did post-doctoral studies in Europe on a Sheldon Traveling Fellowship. He stayed one year in Germany—Berlin and Hamburg—and another in Cambridge, England.

The exposure to Gestalt psychology and the emphasis on individual personhood that he encountered in Germany profoundly influenced Allport. On his return to the United States, he felt somewhat "out of touch" with the prevalent attitudes of the American psychological community. His European stay stimulated another significant quality in his professional work. Throughout his life, he had strong intercultural and interdisciplinary interests, which he also instilled in his students.

Allport began his academic career as an instructor at Harvard where, it is assumed, he taught the **first course on personality in this country.** After two years, he accepted a professorship in psychology at Dartmouth College but returned to Harvard in 1930 and remained there for the rest of his life. Throughout his career, Allport was respected as educator and researcher who made major contributions to the fields of personality theory, social psychology, and ethics. In 1965 he went into semiretirement and died two years later of cancer.

MAIN POINTS OF EMPHASIS IN ALLPORT'S THEORY

Eclecticism

Most theories discussed up to this point had a central theme, which provided the interpretation of all functions of personality, e.g., the pleasure principle of Freud or the striving for superiority theme of Adler. Others used one basic process to explain all personality functioning, such as Dollard and Miller's stimulus-response sequence or Skinner's operant conditioning. Allport's personality theory is devoid of such a **unifying factor** but incorporates selected ideas and methods of modern psychology without pledging allegiance to any of them. Allport frequently set diametrically opposite approaches side-by-side and steered a middle course between them.

Philosophy of the Person

Allport was convinced that every theory of personality is based on the **philosophical frame** of reference in which human nature is perceived: "The positivist and psychoanalytic views rest on physicalism or on a somewhat broader naturalism. The personalitistic position in its various forms has ties with German idealism, with Protestant theology, or with Thomistic thought. . . . And so it goes with all the formulations" (Allport, 1961, pp. 566–567).

Because of this conviction, Allport encouraged students of personality theory to be aware of the philosophical consequences they accept by adhering to one or another psychological interpretation.

The Empirical-Humanistic Approach

Learning about human behavior and **respect** for the individual were Allport's central concerns. He was

> lukewarm toward models that render personality in terms of giant computing machines, mathematical and statistical constructs, and other simulations. There is no objection to the use of such models for explorative research. Damage is

done only when devotees claim that their approach yields accounts "more fundamental" than does an empirical-humanistic approach (Allport, 1961, p. xi.)

Closely linked with this emphasis is Allport's determination to focus on the **uniqueness of every person** rather than merely on uniform patterns in human nature. His theory balanced the prevalent **nomothetic approach,** formulating universal principles, with the less prevalent **idiographic approach** that considers the uniqueness of persons and situations. Allport favored the idiographic approach.

NATURE OF PERSONALITY

Allport (1961) refuted the concept of personality as a mere inference of behavior. He viewed it as something real in people and argued: "Personality **is** something and **does** something" (p. 29). This statement is a verbatim repetition of what he wrote twenty-five years earlier (Allport, 1937) and indicates the firmness of his commitment to this fundamental tenet.

Before presenting the text of Allport's definition of personality, I want to point out some of its salient components: (1) Personality is a **dynamic** structure that has to be seen in the process of **becoming.** No matter what the age of the individual, personality is never a finished outcome of that process. (2) Personality is **psychophysical** in nature. This entails the combined functioning of mind and body. Personality is not exclusively linked with either neural or physical processes. (3) Everything the individual does is summarized by Allport as **characteristic behavior and thought.** It includes all external and internal processes required for everyday coping, for physiological and social survival, and for personal growth and self-fulfillment.

Allport (1961) defined personality as follows: "Personality is the dynamic organization within the individual of those psychophysical systems that determine his characteristic behavior and thought" (p. 28).

Temperament and Character

Like Fromm, Allport (1961) perceived two aspects of personality: temperament and character. Temperament is "the raw material from which personality is fashioned," whereas character has an ethical, value-related dimension; it is "personality evaluated" (p. 33). Temperament and character should be seen, however, as mere **facets of personality,** not some special regions within it.

Individual Freedom

On the issue of personal freedom, Allport steered a **middle course** between the position of total freedom claimed by existentialism and total lack of freedom postulated by determinism. Individuals are free to chart their lives but only to a degree. They cannot free themselves from their physiological needs, from the influences of earlier learning and experiences, nor from the ongoing influences of the environment. In spite of the constraints, however, every individual is able to creatively employ all these forces to forge a personal life-style: "The basic existentialist urge to grow, pursue meaning, seek unity is also a given. It is a major fact—even more prominent in man's nature than his propensity to yield to surrounding pressures. It is this desire for autonomy, for individuation, for selfhood, for existential uniqueness that enters into the shaping of the product" (Allport, 1961, p. 563).

THE PROPRIUM AND PERSONALITY DEVELOPMENT

The concept of the **proprium** (a Latin adjective meaning "one's own") was developed by Allport (1955, 1961) to explain the **evolving sense of the self** and the processes of **personality development.** He pointed out that his explanation of personality development differs from the stimulus-response theory, but is closely related to views focusing on the self or ego:

> Our position, in brief, is this: all psychological functions commonly ascribed to a self or ego must be admitted as data in the scientific study of personality. These functions are not, however, coextensive with personality as a whole. They are rather the special aspects of personality that have to do with warmth, with unity, with a sense of personal importance. In this exposition I have called them "propriate" functions. (Allport, 1955, p. 55)

Allport outlined the development of the self in terms of eight **propriate functions** that range from simple to more complex processes. The propriate functions are explained here in separate units. Each unit first defines the specific function and, in the second paragraph, applies it to the corresponding developmental stage of the self.

1. The Sense of One's Body

The sense of one's body involves **muscular** and **visceral reactions** (gut feelings), along with other sensations that originate in the organism.

Through the bodily sense, the infant experiences the first aspect of selfhood. The use of eyesight is very important at this stage, since it facilitates spatial perception and helps the infant discover that there is a difference between "my body" and outside objects. Allport (1955) suggested this simple experiment to underscore his point: "Think first of swallowing the saliva in your mouth, or do so. Then imagine expectorating it into a tumbler and drinking it! What seemed natural and 'mine' suddenly becomes disgusting and alien" (p. 43).

2. Self-Identity

Identity is bound with one's **continuity** from day-to-day, e.g., remembering one's thoughts and actions from yesterday and from a week ago, and realizing that the past thoughts and actions belong to the same person.

The child develops the sense of self-identity gradually. At first, "the child readily surrenders his identity in play. He may lose it so completely that he grows angry if other people fail to recognize him as a bear, an airplane, or whatever his fantasy has wrought" (Allport, 1961, p. 116).

3. Ego-Enhancement

Allport (1955) called ego-enhancement "the most notorious property of the proprium" that usually connotes "unabashed self seeking.... And yet, self-love may be prominent in our natures without necessarily being sovereign" (pp. 44–45).

In the second and third year of life, the child explores the environment, gets into things and shows autonomy and a **degree of pride**. The greatest disappointment for the child is to be put to shame.

4. Self-Extension

By identifying with another person, group, or cause, a person extends the range of **self-involvement**. In Allport's view, self-involvement in abstract ideals is a mark of adult maturity.

A child of four to six years of age experiences self-extension at a more basic level. During this stage the child makes a clear delineation of the self while identifying with others; he or she considers dad, mother, a brother or a sister, the dog, and the family home as "belonging to me."

5. Rational Coper

This aspect of the proprium identifies the source of **reasoning** and **coping behaviors** in a person. Virtually all theories recognize a rational agent in personality, even such philosophical antagonists as psychoanalysis and the Christian philosophy of Thomism (named after its originator, Thomas Aquinas). Freud recognized the need for a rational reconciliation of instinctual demands with reality through the secondary process. Thomism considers the primacy of reason over feelings and passions to be one of its dominant principles.

This stage and the next roughly coincide with the time a child spends in elementary school (ages 6 to 12). Allport (1961) considered the developmental processes related to these two propriate functions as interrelated. The child that in the past merely thought about extraneous things now becomes **aware** of his or her own thinking and develops the ability of being introspective. The emerging rational coping indicates a significant development of the ego.

6. Self-Image

The concept of self-image is similar to Cattell's sentiment of self or to the self-concept as used in phenomenology and self-theory (to be discussed in the next two chapters). It involves the way a person feels about him or herself (**real self**) and a person's idea of what he or she would like to become (**ideal self**).

At this stage the child often experiences unkind treatment by his or her classmates, who are eager to point out weaknesses of others and ridicule them. The child learns that peer society greatly differs from the family. He or she wants to be liked and rigidly follows the rules of peer society: "Parental rules are important, but the rules of the gang are utterly binding. The child does not yet trust itself to be an independent moral agent" (Allport, 1961, p. 123).

7. Propriate Striving

This facet of the proprium relates to **motivation.** In Allport's (1955) view, propriate striving is not geared toward tension reduction: "The characteristic feature of such striving is its resistance to equilibrium: tension is maintained rather than reduced" (p. 49). This kind of motivation produces a "unification of personality" and involves planning, interests, problem solving, and other related functions.

Processes of this stage are roughly parallel to Erikson's discovery of self-identity. The youth's initial striving is but marginally propriate; as maturity prevails, however, the young person develops a unified goal orientation that leads to a true propriate striving in adulthood.

8. The Self as Knower

Whereas William James believed that "the thoughts themselves are the thinker," Allport (1955) argued otherwise. The "I" is the ultimate monitor or knower of intrapersonal processes; in fact, "the self as **knower** emerges as a final and inescapable postulate" (p. 52).

This stage involves the development of self-awareness, value orientation, and the formation of a philosophy of life. Allport (1961) emphasizes that an adult is able to be self-objective, to possess **insight** and **humor.** Insight is best understood as the matching of what a person thinks of self and what others think of him or her. Humor "is the ability to laugh at the things one loves (including, of course, oneself and all that pertains to oneself) and still to love them" (Allport, 1961, p. 292).

TRAITS AND PERSONAL DISPOSITIONS

In discussing traits in general and common traits in particular (see Chap. 8), Allport (1961) emphasized the **uniqueness** of each individual (idiographic orientation). He resisted the notion that living human beings should be forced "into a uniform schedule of traits" which express behavioral characteristics of a large number of people. Instead, he coined the term **personal disposition.** Whereas a common trait is a mere abstraction of a typical behavior pattern, the person's disposition is unique and relatively consistent.

Personal dispositions are arranged according to a hierarchy:

1. **Cardinal dispositions.** Allport's (1961) explanation of this concept proves his interest in unusual persons:

> Occasionally some personal disposition is so pervasive and so outstanding in a life that it deserves to be called a **cardinal** disposition. Almost every act seems traceable to its influence.... No such disposition can remain hidden, an individual is known by it, and may become famous for it. Such a master quality has sometimes been called the **eminent trait,** the **ruling passion,** the **master-sentiment,** the **unity-thema,** or the **radix** of a life. (p. 365.)

Cardinal dispositions are present in the lives of relatively few persons.

2. **Central and secondary dispositions.** These dispositions mark the behavior of most people. **Central dispositions** are of major importance to the individual, are conspicuous, and are consistent. Allport assumed that a handful of these dispositions would outline the focal points of a person's general behavior. Central dispositions are identical with the characteristics of a person usually listed in a well-written letter of recommendation.

Secondary dispositions are less important for the individual, less conspicuous, and less consistent from one situation of life to another. We could perceive them as complementary to the central dispositions in everyday life as occasions may warrant.

FUNCTIONAL AUTONOMY

Functional autonomy is a concept developed and frequently discussed by Allport (1955, 1960, 1961, 1968) in his writings. **Motivation** is always **in the present;** yet, behavior initiated in the past for a particular purpose is frequently maintained without properly understanding its original purpose: "The activity once served a drive or some simple need; it now serves itself" (Allport, 1961, p. 229).

Functional autonomy can have a negative connotation, but it can be turned into a creative effort:

1. **Perseverative functional autonomy** is, simply said, a **meaningless routine,** a shell without content; it may be an addiction to social customs and may even turn into addiction to social abuses, including chemical substance abuse. Fundamentally, it is a mechanistic behavior without intrinsic value called by Allport a "low-grade process."

For instance, in Mexico peasants passing a church make the sign of the cross and then kiss their hand. The latter part of this symbolic act is meaningless for them, since they are no longer aware of the old instruction of missionaries; they were to form a small cross by crossing their thumb and forefinger and to kiss it. In the missionaries' view, this devotional act would provide people with spiritual benefits. The current habit, however, is maintained merely because of social reinforcement and amounts to a meaningless routine.

2. **Propriate functional autonomy** is a process by which an earlier-developed behavior is given a **new meaning.** Propriate striving, the unifying element in personality, can fill the empty shell of functional autonomy with authentic content. For instance, a handshake—in early times the sign of peaceful intentions of a person who was not armed—can be turned into a warm expression of friendship by a person of genuine character.

APPLICATIONS TO COUNSELING

Allport's theory contains a number of basic approaches and concepts that may be directly applicable to counseling practice, for example:

1. The need for a clear philosophy of human nature
2. The appreciation of the uniqueness of every person
3. Allport's concept of personality in its genetic and value-related aspects (temperament and character)
4. His view of individual freedom
5. The proprium and its application to human development
6. The concept of personal dispositions
7. The two kinds of functional autonomy

CHAPTER REVIEW

1. How did Allport's life experiences affect the development of his theory?
2. What is Allport's concept of systematic eclecticism?
3. Which are the main points of Allport's theory?
4. How does Allport define personality, and what differentiation does he make between temperament and character?
5. What is Allport's view of human freedom?
6. What is meant by the proprium, and which are its eight functions?
7. Which major implications of the proprium on personality development do you recall?

8. How does Allport perceive the development of self-identity in the child?
9. What is meant by self-objectivity in a mature adult?
10. What is Allport's view of common traits, and what is the nature and hierarchy of personal dispositions in his theory?
11. What is meant by functional autonomy, and which two kinds of functional autonomy do you know?
12. Which of Allport's concepts and recommended attitudes do you consider useful for present-day counseling?

REFERENCES

Allport, G. W. (1955). *Becoming: Basic considerations for a psychology of personality.* New Haven, CT: Yale University Press.

Allport, G. W. (1954). *The nature of prejudice.* Reading, MA: Addison-Wesley.

Allport, G. W. (1961). *Patterns and growth in personality.* New York: Holt, Rinehart & Winston.

Allport, G. W. (1968). *The person in psychology: Selected essays.* Boston: Beacon Press.

Allport, G. W. (1937). *Personality: A psychological interpretation.* New York: Holt, Rinehart & Winston.

Allport, G. W. (1960). *Personality and social encounter: Selected essays.* Boston: Beacon Press.

Evans, R. I. (1971). *Gordon Allport: The man and his ideas.* New York: Dutton.

CHAPTER 11

PHENOMENOLOGY AND EXISTENTIALISM

PHENOMENOLOGY and existentialism are very closely related, both at the philosophical and at the psychological levels. In fact, some authors, e.g., VanKaam (1966), consider phenomenology to be a method used in various fields, including existentialism. It is not easy to decide whether phenomenology is attached to existentialism or whether existentialism is one of the orientations that are collectively called the phenomenological movement (Misiak & Sexton, 1973).

Phenomenology and existentialism play an important role in what is called "the third force in American psychology," which emerged in opposition to psychoanalysis and behaviorism. The personality theories to be discussed in Chapters 12–14 also belong to this general orientation.

Because of the nature of the subject matter covered in this chapter, a clarification is in order: Phenomenology is presented as it evolved from its philosophical roots into a **psychological system.** Existentialism, however, is treated exclusively as a **philosophical movement** that undergirds a number of personality theories.

The chapter outline deviates from the organization of previous chapters. It contains the following units: (1) To facilitate a clear understanding of the difference between philosophy and psychology, a way of separating the two fields of study is suggested at the outset. (2) Existentialism, the philosophical basis of phenomenology, is explained in terms of its origins and basic assumptions. (3) Other sources that contributed to the formation of phenomenological psychology are presented next: Edmund Husserl's philosophy and Gestalt psychology. (4) Finally, a phenomenological model of personality theory is outlined.

PHILOSOPHY AND PSYCHOLOGY

To understand the differences between philosophy and psychology, we will place their definitions side-by-side to draw comparisons and identify contrasts:

1. Psychology is the study of human behavior; its field is **clearly** outlined, but it is **limited** in scope. Psychology does not intend to offer answers to the most profound questions of human life.

2. The definition of philosophy is not that clear or unequivocal. In fact, since the time of relative unity of Western culture in the Middle Ages, many definitions of philosophy sprung up, depending on the school of thought in which each of them originated. Nevertheless, we can formulate a **general definition** incorporating many of the past and current ideas: Philosophy consists of the critical examination, analysis, and interpretation of **fundamental human concerns** (e.g., the nature of being and existence, the person's place in the universe, and the nature of cognition and will), of human **values,** and **ethics.**

Whereas psychology explains observable behavior and intrapersonal dynamics, philosophy endeavors to form a meaningful perspective on human existence in general and on the individual's existence in particular. The concerns of philosophy are of a deeper, ontological nature than those of psychology. This helps us understand why every theory of personality is based on some philosophical assumption about the **nature of man.** Phenomenology, along with other theories, is based on existential philosophy (see Fig. 15).

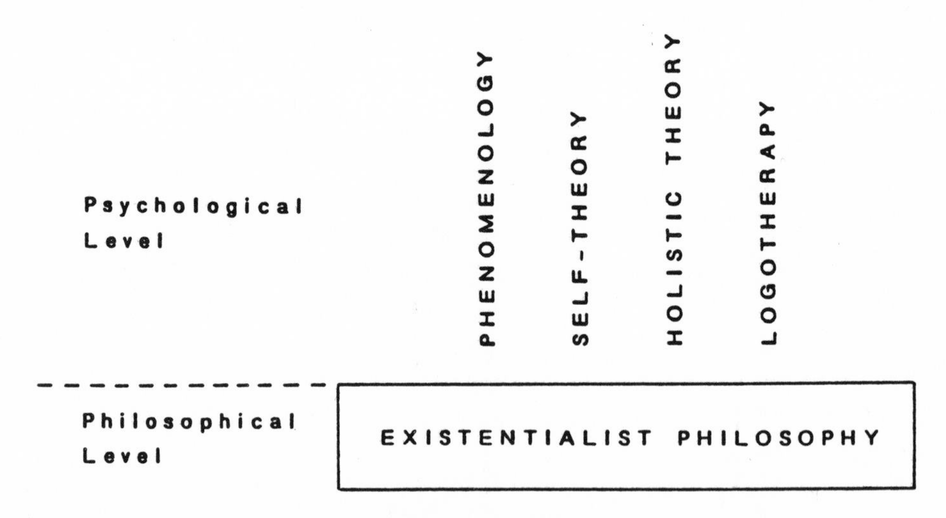

Figure 15. Relationship of certain psychological schools and existential philosophy.

EXISTENTIAL PHILOSOPHY

Existential philosophy (or existentialism) had its origins in the first part of the nineteenth century. It received, however, its current level of recognition and acceptance much later—in Europe after World War I and in America only after World War II.

The founder of existentialism was Soren Kierkegaard (1813–1855), a Danish philosopher and religious thinker. In his view, every individual has the right to freely choose his or her own truth on the subjective basis of faith rather than on the authority of a religious institution. Kierkegaard recognized three "spheres of existence" in human life; the aesthetic, ethical, and religious spheres in which to exercise free and mature choices.

Kierkegaard was highly critical of the religious establishment of his society. In his view, the state church was merely a comfortable compromise between Christianity and social power. Because Kierkegaard (1959, 1962) was ahead of his time, his views found little acceptance at first and he was frequently ridiculed.

Contemporary existentialism is **neutral** in terms of religious faith. Some of its prominent adherents are religious believers, e.g., Gabriel Marcel, Paul Tillich, Rudolf Bultmann, and Martin Buber. Others are agnostics or atheists, e.g., Karl Jaspers, Martin Heidegger, Jean-Paul Sartre, and Albert Camus. No matter what their attitude toward religion may be, their philosophical persuasion is strikingly similar. Even those existentialists who are members of organized religion reject rigid dogmatism and perceive faith as a personal choice or an existential leap into the unknown rather than a response to impelling theological arguments.

Points of Emphasis in Existentialism

1. Existentialism is **not** a philosophical **system** but a philosophical movement. Philosophical systems are contrary to the nature of existentialism because systems shackle the spontaneity of existential experiences.

2. Existentialism rejects past philosophical categories of essence (**what** things are) and existence (**that** they are). It focuses exclusively on existence, which is the **only reality** for every person. A person does not just **possess** existence; a person **is** his or her own existence.

3. Existentialism tolerates a variety of views in its ranks that range from **optimistic** to **tragic**, almost despairing perspectives on human life.

They share, however, certain common assumptions, which are presented here:

a. Every person is in the world, in a particular time and situation. This condition typical of all humans is often called **thereness** (Dasein). It is up to the person to participate in that situation and thus immerse him or herself in existence rather than merely observe it.

b. Every person needs to **create** his or her life (way of life) that is **unique** and **genuine** (honest). Every person has an opportunity to do so because he or she is **free** to choose.

c. Freedom brings about **aloneness.** Free decisions are made at times in company with others, but others cannot share in the process of decision making. His or her closest friend may have offered advice, but the person alone decides **whether** or **how** to use the advice.

d. The sense of aloneness is combined with a sense of **responsibility.** Even decisions that are made in total privacy are made "for the world." By the genuineness of his or her decision a person enhances him or herself and the environment, generating a healthy ethical atmosphere. By a dishonest decision, no matter how private, the person damages his or her own self and generates an ethically unhealthy atmosphere.

e. Human existence is **fragile** in a world, which is open to chance. Human fragility—the contingency of one's being—is a fact of life; whenever the awareness of it enters consciousness, the person experiences **existential anxiety** (Angst).

f. A person can, however, also experience profound joy and fulfillment by genuine relationships with others. Marcel (1952) and Buber (1970) spoke of the I–Thou relationships, which are intersubjective—occurring between two subjects of **equal dignity.** Through such relationships a person shares him or herself with another.

g. In contrast to genuine human relationships, some people engage in I-it relationships by which one person treats another as an **object,** in a manipulative way. Such relationships are degrading for both sides.

h. Existentialism argues that in a world where people are perceived primarily as **functional units** it is difficult to live a genuine life. Marcel (1967) voiced this concern:

> Life in a world centered upon the idea of function is exposed to despair, because in reality this world is empty, because it rings hollow; if it resists despair, it is solely to the extent that certain secret powers, which it is unable to

conceive or to recognize, are at work at the heart of this existence and in its favor. (p. 139.)

THE PHILOSOPHY OF EDMUND HUSSERL

Edmund Husserl (1848–1938) was born in Moravia (today's Czech Republic) and from youth was attracted to the study of mathematics and natural sciences. He earned a doctoral degree in mathematics at the University of Vienna. His postdoctoral work, which he did under Franz Brentano, convinced him, however, that his life's vocation was in the field of philosophy rather than in mathematics.

Husserl's academic career extended over forty-two years, the last thirteen spent at the University of Freiburg in the Black Forest. He was a prolific lecturer and writer. In addition to his published books, he left behind a large number of manuscripts—47,000 pages in shorthand and 12,000 typewritten pages. Over twenty volumes of these materials were published posthumously.

Husserl's Main Philosophical Theme

The primary question formulated by Husserl was identical with what philosophers were asking for centuries: How does **objective reality** relate to the world of thought in the **human mind**? Husserl's response can be summarized as follows: (1) All reality (persons and inanimate things) that exists in our environment can be perceived by us. (2) The process of perception occurs on the basis of an individual's **subjective intuition**, consciousness, and intentionality. (3) The things "out there" are experienced by a person as **phenomena.** (4) These phenomena reveal to the observer the essence of each perceived thing. (5) To understand the full meaning of phenomena, it is necessary to explore the observer's consciousness. (6) A relationship exists between phenomena, actions, and the self of the observer.

Although Bochenski (1961) likened Husserl's philosophy "to a transcendental idealism, in many ways similar to that of Neo-Kantians" (p. 140), it may be more appropriate to call it a theory of cognition based on intuition and blended with a heavy dose of subjectivity. As we shall see, Husserl's philosophical principles are reflected in psychological phenomenology (Husserl, 1977) and in its interpretation of personality.

GESTALT PSYCHOLOGY

Gestalt psychology originated in Germany during the second half of the nineteenth century; its tenets were expounded by two of its founders, Wolfgang Koehler (1964) and Kurt Koffka (1935). Gestalt psychology and phenomenology have much in common and have influenced each other over the years.

One of the more important concepts of Gestalt psychology that has become prominent in phenomenology is **differentiation.** Differentiation is the process of separating figure (the German term for figure is "Gestalt") from ground—a process that occurs again and again in our lives but escapes our awareness. Whatever object we differentiate from a configuration of objects emerges into figure while the other objects fade into ground. It should be noted that differentiation leads to **perception,** and perception leads to **behavior.**

For example, a teenage boy goes to a dance with a couple of other boys. As he surveys the dance hall, he notices a group of girls chatting on the other side of the hall and notices a tall brunette (he differentiates her from the cluster of girls). No matter whether he knows who she is, the boy has by now acquired awareness (perception) of the girl and he will ask her for a dance (behavior). The same process is being applied in all our conscious choices. These choices are free since, at the level of differentiation, we are **free to select** any object available to us. Once we have differentiated a particular object and brought it to the level of figure, our perception and behavioral response follow.

For a better understanding of the process of differentiation, see Figure 16. If the drawing is perceived in its totality, it looks like an unusually shaped vase. If we differentiate, however, the lines on the sides of the vase, we perceive two faces. They emerge into figure and the vase lapses into ground.

A PHENOMENOLOGICAL APPROACH TO PERSONALITY

Some fifty years ago, two American psychologists, Donald Snygg (1904–1967) and Arthur W. Combs (B. 1912) proposed a personality theory from the phenomenological perspective. In 1941 Snygg authored an article on this subject for the *Psychological Review.* It was the first such paper published in American psychological literature. In 1949 Snygg and Combs published their volume, *Individual Behavior: A New Frame of*

Figure 16. An aid to understanding the differentiation process.

Reference for Psychology, that offered a phenomenological interpretation of personality functioning (Misiak & Sexton, 1973). Ten years later, Combs and Snygg (1959) authored a revised edition of the book.

We can better assess the importance of Combs and Snygg's pioneering work as we consider the statement of Hall and Lindzey (1978):

> One of the most articulate and sophisticated contemporary phenomenologists is Erwin Straus (1963, 1966).... [However,] phenomenology, as represented in the works of the Gestalt psychologists and of Erwin Straus, has been employed primarily for investigating the phenomena of such psychological processes as perceiving, learning, remembering, thinking, and feeling, but has not been used in personality studies. (p. 313)

This void has been quite effectively filled by the contributions of Combs and Snygg (1949, 1959). The latter version of their book has served as a major resource for the following section of the present chapter.

PERCEPTUAL FIELD

Phenomenology views personality from the **perceptual frame of reference.** It endeavors to see behavior through the eyes of the behaving person rather than through outside observation or assessment. This is best achieved by the study of the person's perceptual (or phenomenal) field. Combs and Snygg (1959) explained: "By the perceptual field we mean the entire universe, including himself, as it is perceived by the individual at the instant of action" (p. 20). The nature of the perceptual field is **subjective.** Some of the perceptions may be inaccurate; nevertheless, they **seem real** and substantial to the person whose actions they stimulate. For instance, a tumbleweed on a Wyoming country road will be readily recognized at night by a local driver for what it is, whereas a visitor from the East may consider it to be a boulder and warn the driver to stop.

The perceptual field contains an inner region called the perceptual or **phenomenal self.** It is the way people see themselves in various situations in which they are involved: working on their job, playing with a child, studying for an exam, etc. The phenomenal self changes from one situation to another. It is, however, "not a mere conglomeration or addition of isolated concepts, but a patterned interrelationship or Gestalt of all these" (Combs & Snygg, 1959, p. 126).

The core of the phenomenal self is the **self-concept** around which the rest of the perceptual field is formed. In contrast with the phenomenal self, "the self-concept serves as a kind of shorthand approach by which the individual may symbolize and reduce his vast complexity to workable and usable terms" (Combs & Snygg, 1959, p. 127). Whereas the phenomenal self changes from situation to situation, the self-concept remains relatively constant.

One's self-concept has an important bearing on mental health or illness. A **positive** self-concept is the sign of a mentally healthy individual, whereas a **negative** self-concept is associated with maladjustment, depression, and even sociopathic behavior. The structure of the perceptual field can be seen in Figure 17.

Fluidity of the Perceptual Field

Through the process of differentiation, **new perceptions** are formed and enter the phenomenal field. Perceptions of the superficial nature remain on the periphery of the perceptual field. If, however, an important perception enters the perceptual field, it penetrates deep inside; it is perceived as related to the phenomenal self. Peripheral perceptions influence a person's behavior in a minor way; perceptions that penetrate deep into the field become major behavioral determinants.

The acceptance of new perceptions into the perceptual field and the

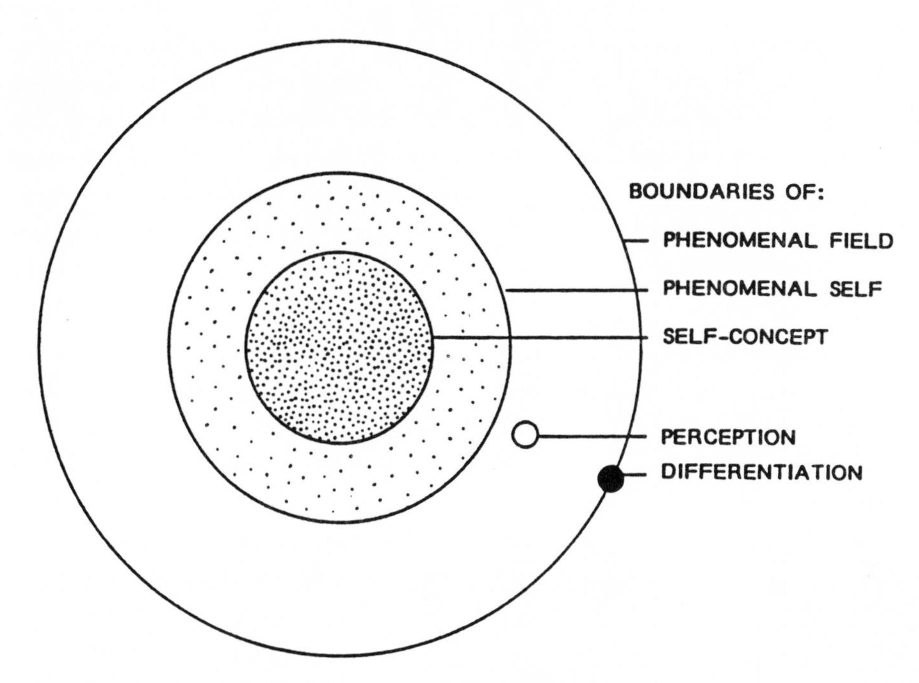

Figure 17. Structure of the perceptual or phenomenal field.

discarding of established perceptions that are no longer perceived to be relevant explain the **gradual changes** in a person's interests and values. The phenomenal self and the self-concept are more resistant to such changes, but they are not immune to them.

MATURATION AND ADEQUACY

The fluidity of the perceptual field is the basis of the maturation process. The motivational force that impels the person to strive for maturity is the basic human **need for adequacy:**

> Man seeks not merely the maintenance of self but the development of an **adequate** self—a self capable of dealing effectively and efficiently with the exigencies of life, both now and in the future. To achieve this self-adequacy requires of man that he seek, not only to maintain his existing organization, but also that he build up and make more adequate the self of which he is aware. (Combs & Snygg, 1959, p. 45.)

An adequate person has achieved a high degree of need satisfaction and effective coping behaviors. Combs and Snygg (1959) list specifically the following characteristics of an adequate person:

1. **Positive self-perception.** Adequate people see themselves more often in "enhancing" rather than "destructive" terms. Despite their awareness of certain negative characteristics of the self, they maintain a sense of inner worth and dignity.

2. **Acceptance of self and others.** A positive self-perception naturally leads to self-acceptance. Adequate persons accept all their experiences as they appear in their perceptual field. Their self-acceptance is intimately linked with the acceptance of others. Acceptance of self and others provides adequate persons with a valuable trait—a willingness to **forgive** themselves and others—since they recognize imperfections and failures to be among the natural threads of the human fabric.

Adequate persons appear to be **well-adjusted**, although they do not make a conscious effort to conform. They refuse to bow to convention and do not worry how society will evaluate them. With regard to ethical issues, Combs and Snygg (1959) pointed out that "compassion, understanding, responsibility, and humility are not blindly sought as desirable goals for behavior. Rather, such characteristics are a natural outgrowth of the capacities for acceptance and identification" (p. 258).

3. **Relaxed openness to life.** This quality of life counteracts rigidity and facilitates growth through meaningful changes. The perceptual field of adequate persons is both fluid and consistent. They are less defensive about themselves and more effective in their work. Adequate persons are truly creative. Combs and Snygg (1959) add that "the great reservoir of positive perceptions and the capacity for acceptance of self and the world gives the adequate person a tremendous advantage in dealing with life" (p. 250).

EMOTIONAL PROBLEMS

In terms of the perceptual frame of reference, emotional problems are characterized by a breakdown of the processes of differentiation, perception, and acceptance of self: "The ability to perceive and to reorganize the phenomenal field becomes seriously hampered" (Combs & Snygg, 1959, p. 285).

Neurotic patients have a distorted perspective. The distortion is frequently related to the degree of their perceived culpability, unworthiness, or guilt. The negative perception of themselves is exaggerated. Such feelings are likely accompanied by strong attempts to achieve adequacy.

If this struggle is within the limits established by society for acceptable behavior, a person is considered neurotic or maladjusted.

In the view of Combs and Snygg (1959), "when, however, the individual's search for adequacy leads him to behavior threatening or destructive to persons or property, he may be considered delinquent or criminal" (p. 285). In either case the true cause of the behavior problem is to be found in the underlying feeling of **inadequacy.**

APPLICATIONS TO COUNSELING

Several concepts from phenomenology and existentialism are applicable to counseling practice, e.g.:

1. The concept of the perceptual field as the subjective world of the client
2. The concept of adequacy as the outcome of maturation
3. The characterization of an adequate personality
4. The perceptual view of emotional problems
5. Some existential tenets, such as personal freedom and responsibility, human fragility, existential anxiety, and I–Thou relationships

CHAPTER REVIEW

1. What is the difference between psychology and philosophy?
2. What were the origins of existentialism, and did existentialism develop into a philosophical system?
3. What is meant by "thereness" and by our making decisions "for the world"?
4. What is meant by human fragility and existential anxiety?
5. What is meant by I–Thou and I–It relationships?
6. What do you remember about the life of Edmund Husserl?
7. What was the main theme of Husserl's philosophy?
8. What contribution did Gestalt psychology make to phenomenological psychology?
9. How do Combs and Snygg structure the perceptual field, and what difference do they see between the phenomenal self and the self-concept?
10. What is meant by adequacy, and which are the marks of an adequate personality?
11. What is the perceptual explanation of emotional problems?

12. Which concepts proposed by phenomenology and existentialism do you consider applicable to present-day counseling practice?

REFERENCES

Bochenski, I. M. (1961). *Contemporary European philosophy.* Berkeley: University of California Press.

Buber, M. (1970). *I and Thou.* New York: Scribner.

Combs, A. W., & Snygg, D. (1959). *Individual behavior: A perceptual approach to behavior.* New York: Harper & Row.

Hall, C. S., & Lindzey, G. (1978). *Theories of personality* (3rd ed.). New York: Wiley.

Husserl, E. (1977). *Phenomenological psychology: Lectures, summer semester, 1925.* The Hague: Nijhoff.

Kierkegaard, S. (1959). *The journals of Soren Kierkegaard* (A. Dru, Ed.). London: Oxford University Press.

Kierkegaard, S. (1962). *The present age, and Of the difference between a genius and an apostle.* New York: Harper & Row.

Koehler, W. (1964). *Gestalt psychology.* New York: New American Library.

Koffka, K. (1935). *Principles of gestalt psychology.* New York: Harcourt, Brace.

Marcel, G. (1952). *Men against humanity.* London: Harvill.

Marcel, G. (1967). *Problematic man.* New York: Herder & Herder.

Misiak, H., & Sexton, V. S. (1973). *Phenomenological, existential, and humanistic psychologies.* New York: Grune & Stratton.

Straus, E. W. (1966). *Phenomenological psychology: The selected papers of Erwin W. Straus.* New York: Basic Books.

Straus, E. W. (1963). *The primary world of senses: A vindication of sensory experience.* Glencoe, IL: Free Press.

Van Kaam, A. (1966). *Existential foundations of psychology.* Pittsburgh: Duquesne University Press.

CHAPTER 12

SELF-THEORY

CARL R. ROGERS (1902-1987)

CARL ROGERS has exerted a major influence on the helping professions over the past fifty years, both in the United States and abroad. In an environment pervaded by psychoanalytical and behaviorist ideas, he proposed a new approach to counseling: the Client-Centered or Person-Centered Therapy. He also introduced a novel personality theory with the concept of the self at its center, emphasizing the unity and uniqueness of every person. As early as the 1940s, he spoke openly in favor of phenomenology and identified with basic existentialist principles, particularly as they related to freedom of choice and to genuine human relationships.

Instead of depending on diagnostic tools for assessment of personality functioning, Rogers preferred to gather information from the clients themselves. In one of his informal statements, he emphasized that whatever he knew about personality and behavior he had learned from his clients.

ROGERS' LIFE

Carl Ransom Rogers was born in Oak Park, Illinois. His affluent parents were religious conservatives who rarely socialized with neighbors and instilled in their six children a Spartan life-style along with a strong Protestant work ethic. When Carl reached his twelfth year, his father decided to purchase a farm, which he tried to manage according to new agronomical methods. Young Carl read a lot, particularly on agriculture, worked hard on his studies and on his assigned farm chores, but enjoyed virtually none of the recreational activities typical of his age group. This stressful life-style led to health problems; as a teenager, Carl developed an ulcer that was misdiagnosed by a local physician as a "symptom of physiological development." Rogers had to cope with this gastric problem throughout his life.

The years Rogers spent at the University of Wisconsin, where he did his undergraduate work, gave him a new perspective on life. He blossomed in the new atmosphere of academic freedom, which stimulated his intellect and affected his religious views (Rogers, 1959). As a junior he was offered the opportunity to travel with a youth group to China for a world congress of Christian students. The sojourn in China additionally broadened his religious perspective and offered him a new intercultural outlook. While still at Wisconsin, he married a fellow student, Helen Elliott, who was preparing for a career in commercial art.

After Carl's graduation the young couple moved to New York where Rogers enrolled at the Union Theological Seminary. Eventually, he transferred to Teachers College at Columbia University and earned his doctorate in psychology there. His first job as staff psychologist at a child guidance clinic in Rochester, New York, brought Rogers a sudden change from the measurement-oriented environment at Columbia to the psychoanalytic orientation of his new colleagues.

After twelve years of clinical practice in Rochester, Rogers transferred to Ohio State University. This was a significant shift in his professional development; he moved from purely clinical concerns to basic theoretical formulations that crystallized out of his experiences. This development was additionally intensified after Rogers transferred to the University of Chicago and, later, when he moved on to the University of Wisconsin to accept there a joint appointment as professor of psychology and psychiatry. Combining clinical work with research was typical of most of Rogers' academic pursuits. At Wisconsin he added, however, a new dimension by agreeing to head a large clinical team that researched outcomes of therapy in the treatment of psychotic patients in several area hospitals.

Rogers resigned his professorship at the University of Wisconsin in opposition to the practice of "weeding out" a quota of doctoral students admitted to advanced graduate work in psychology. Since 1964 he lived in California, at first associated with the Western Behavioral Science Institute, later serving as resident fellow of the Center for the Study of the Person at La Jolla, an institute that he himself founded.

POINTS OF EMPHASIS IN ROGERS' THEORY

Humanism and Existentialism

Rogers was strongly committed to protecting the **personhood** of people in the humanist tradition. In this context, he defended humanism against those who portray it as a pseudo-religious movement called "secular humanism," which they consider to be the cause of various social ills, such as sexual promiscuity, drug abuse, and delinquency.

Rogers (1961, 1983) espoused many existentialist views, particularly the dual emphasis on **existence** (versus essence) and **freedom:** (1) Self-theory perceives every person as a **process** rather than a completed product. (2) Although constrained by social norms in overt actions, every person needs to exercise **freedom.** This particularly applies to his or her thinking processes (Rogers called thinking or awareness "symbolization") and to the accompanying emotions: "To destroy a hated object (whether one's mother or a rococo building) by destroying a symbol of it, is freeing" (Rogers, 1961, p. 359). No doubt, Rogers projected here his own feelings of exuberance when he first experienced true freedom in the college atmosphere after years of regimented home life.

Optimistic View of Human Nature

Rogers (1961) had a highly optimistic view of the organism—the basis of all human experiences, which he considered to be frequently **wiser** than the person's awareness:

> I have little sympathy with the rather prevalent concept that man is basically irrational, and that his impulses, if not controlled, will lead to destruction of others and self. Man's behavior is exquisitely rational, moving with subtle and ordered complexity toward the goals his organism is endeavoring to achieve. The tragedy for most of us is that our defenses keep us from being aware of this rationality, so that consciously we are moving in one direction, while organismically we are moving in another. (pp. 194–195.)

This boundless optimism of Rogers has been criticized from various quarters as overstated and unrealistic. Among the critics were many psychologists, some of whom considered Rogers's ideas a naive misapplication of phenomenology (cf. Smith, 1950).

Opposition to Behaviorism

Rogers (1961) did not perceive behaviorist approaches to be helpful for studying or promoting personality development. He expressed "a deep concern that the developing behavioral sciences may be used to control the individual and rob him of his personhood" (p. 361). People have a choice to let behavioral sciences make them happy, well-behaved, docile, submissive, and conforming. People have, of course, also the choice to maintain their freedom and strive for creative **variability rather than conformity.** Responsible personal choices constitute the crucial element of personhood.

It should be added that, in recent years, Rogers (1977) favorably commented on the gradual change in attitudes of many behaviorists who interpret Skinner's doctrine in a humanistic context.

STUDY OF PERSONALITY: INTERNAL FRAME OF REFERENCE

In his book, *Client-centered therapy,* Rogers (1951) summarized his personality theory in nineteen propositions. Along with the accompanying comments, these propositions form the basis for a clear understanding of his theoretical framework.

In explaining the structure of personality, Rogers's theory closely resembles the phenomenological model discussed in the previous chapter. Rogers (1951), too, used the perceptual (he called it **internal**) frame of reference to see things from the vantage point of the observed person rather than through the eyes of an objective outsider.

The internal frame of reference is an **attitude** rather than a technique. To "walk in the moccasins of another" is not easy. The professional has to be willing to gather information on the inner world of the subject by means of the subject's verbal and nonverbal messages, not through objective assessment.

BASIC HUMAN MOTIVATION

Every individual has a basic tendency and striving for **self-actualization** that includes a number of needs, e.g. for food, security, independence, self-directiveness, and fulfillment through genuine interpersonal relationships. Behavior is always motivated by **current** needs, not by past events, although they may affect motivation to some degree.

The thrust of the drive for self-actualization and the ensuing goal-oriented behavior intensify to the degree that the individual is "inwardly free." Self actualization efforts are accompanied by **emotions**, which increase in strength the more a person recognizes the significance of his or her striving:

> The individual is becoming more able to listen to himself, to experience what is going on within himself. He is more open to his feelings of fear and discouragement and pain. He is also more open to his feelings of courage, and tenderness, and awe. He is free to live his feelings subjectively, as they exist to him, and also free to be aware of these feelings. (Rogers, 1961, p. 188.)

THE ORGANISM

The phenomenal field contains two components, which can be differentiated in terms of their respective functions, but are not separated like two distinct parts of the whole.

The **organism** is the psychophysical basis of all experiences. These include thought processes, desires, emotions, visceral reactions, and various types of overt behavior. Some of these experiences may be pleasurable, others painful or threatening. Rogers (1951) viewed the organism as an "organized whole" that accepts all experiences present in the phenomenal field comprising the person's subjective reality at any given moment.

The organism, however, is not only a recipient of experiences; it is also the locus of the earlier-discussed drive for self-enhancement through need satisfaction. In Rogers's (1951) view, needs are specific types of physiological tension. Tension stimulates behavior, which is likely to result in tension reduction and growth of the organism.

The **striving** for self-actualization through need fulfillment and the **receptivity** to experiences as they exist in the phenomenal field are the two important functions of the organism.

THE SELF

The **self** is the second component of the phenomenal field. It emerges gradually: "As the infant develops, a portion of the total private world becomes recognized as 'me,' 'I,' 'myself.' There are many puzzling and unanswered questions in regard to the dawning concept of the self" (Rogers, 1951, p. 497).

The first step in explaining the Rogerian concept of the self may be to clarify what the self **does.** The self relates to the experiences that are present in the organism. When dealing with such experiences, the self can do one of the following three things: (1) symbolize and accept them as part of the self; (2) deny them because they are not consistent with the structure of the self; or (3) symbolize them in a **distorted** manner; this occurs when "concepts and values are introjected from parents and others in the environment, but are perceived in the phenomenal field as being the product of sensory evidence" (Rogers, 1951, p. 525).

In Rogers's (1983) view, to find one's real self is an arduous task. It means that people have to muster their courage to "move away from hiding behind facades and pretenses . . . toward a greater closeness to, and awareness of, what they are inwardly experiencing . . . ranging from wild and 'crazy' feelings to solid, socially approved ones" (p. 39).

PSYCHOLOGICAL HEALTH AND MALADJUSTMENT

On the basis of the previous section, we will understand Rogers's (1951) interpretation of psychological health and maladjustment. Psychological **health** "exists when the concept of the self is such that all the sensory and visceral experiences of the organism are, or may be, assimilated . . . with the concept of self" (p. 513). A well-adjusted person accepts "ownership" of all his or her organismic experiences. The diagram of a well-adjusted personality can be found in Figure 18.

In Rogers's (1951) view, "psychological maladjustment exists when the organism denies to awareness significant sensory and visceral experiences" (p. 510) since they are too threatening to the self-structure. This **denial** can occur either at the conscious level or below the level needed for conscious recognition. Rogers (1951, 1961) calls this process "subception" and places it outside of the person's awareness.

The more threatening the experiences, the greater the rigidity of the self-structure. The resulting intrapersonal situation is quite damaging because of the "discrepancy between the experiencing organism as it exists, and the concept of self which exerts such a governing influence upon behavior" (Rogers, 1951, pp. 510–511). A maladjusted person is unable or unwilling to accept ownership of his or her experiences. The diagram of a maladjusted personality can be found in Figure 19.

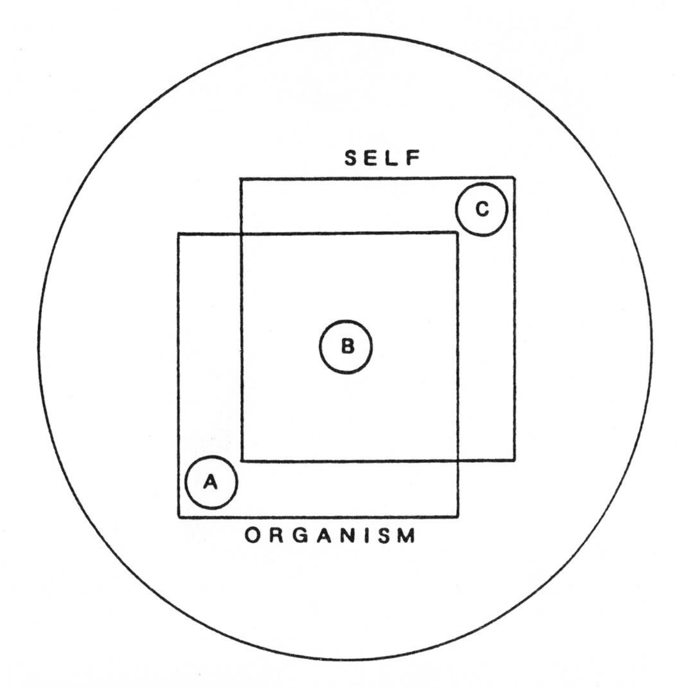

A--DENIED EXPERIENCES
B--ACCURATELY SYMBOLIZED EXPERIENCES (AREA OF CONGRUENCE)
C--EXPERIENCES SYMBOLIZED IN A DISTORTED MANNER

Figure 18. Rogers's view of a well-adjusted personality.

CONGRUENCE

An important concept in Rogerian theory is **congruence;** its absence or the relative lack of it is called **incongruence.**

Congruence is defined as the **matching** of experiences as they are present in the **organism** and as they are symbolized in the **self.** The symbolization must be accurate, without distortion, to produce a state of congruence of experience and self (Rogers, 1959).

Incongruence is the **lack** of accurate symbolization of organismic experiences in the self. It is a discrepancy between one's experiences and one's perceptions of such experiences, resulting in a slanted awareness of self.

A high degree of congruence is a mark of mental health in the person; a low degree of congruence is indicative of maladjustment. In Figures 18 and 19 the contrasting degrees of congruence are indicated by the varied

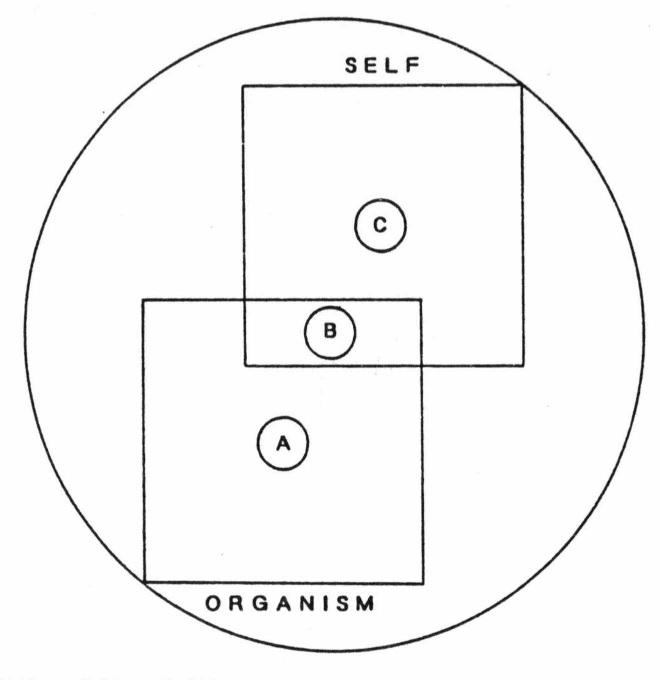

A--DENIED EXPERIENCES
B--ACCURATELY SYMBOLIZED EXPERIENCES (AREA OF CONGRUENCE)
C--EXPERIENCES SYMBOLIZED IN A DISTORTED MANNER

Figure 19. Rogers's view of a maladjusted personality.

overlap of the two squares representing the organism and the self. Parenthetically, it should be noted that Rogers (1961) emphasized congruence in the counselor's personality as one of the important conditions for successful therapy.

DEVELOPMENT OF THE SELF-CONCEPT

The self-concept reflects a person's view of him or herself: in positive, enhancing terms or in negative, demeaning terms. To a large extent, the self-concept is **molded** by a person's parents and other significant persons early in life. Unconditional positive regard shown to the child facilitates the formation of a positive self-concept, which is correlated with a high degree of congruence between experiences and the self. Parental caring without any conditions attached makes it unnecessary for the child to deny any of his or her experiences. This high degree of congruence leads to psychological adjustment.

A child who has not received unconditional positive regard and who has occasionally received negative messages about him or herself (compare with Sullivan's "good me" and "bad me" personifications in Chapter 5) feels the need to **deny** some of the experiences in the organism as unacceptable. This leads to incongruence in the child's personality and to maladjustment in later life. Since he or she tries to conform to other people's wishes rather than express his or her own self, such a person develops behavior patterns, which in Rogers's view are quite unhealthy.

Rogers (1959) made a case for striving toward an unconditional positive **self-regard**, which emerges "when the individual perceives himself in such a way that no self-experience can be discriminated as more or less worthy of positive regard than any other" (p. 209).

THE IDEAL AND THE REAL SELF

Most people differentiate the image of what they hope to become (**ideal self**) from what they believe they are (**real self**). In most cases the difference is not significant. In maladjusted persons, however, there is virtually no similarity between the two self-concepts.

In his clinical work, Rogers (1951) used the **Q-technique** developed by William Stephenson to study the relationship of the perceived ideal and real selves in clients before and after therapy. The Q-technique consists of the patient sorting cards containing various statements, some positive, others negative, typically made by clients before and after therapy.

In the **self-sort** the subject is asked to sort the cards on a continuum beginning with statements that are "least like you." The same is also done in the **ideal-sort.** The two series of statements are then correlated. Rogers and his associates used this approach to engage in research on the effects of therapy.

THE GOOD LIFE

Rogers (1961) described a "fully functioning person" and coined the term of "good life" as the mode of living of such people. In many ways his description of the good life is merely a summary of many of the principles presented in his other writings.

In Rogers's (1961) view, "the good life is a **process,** not a state of being. It is a direction, not a destination. The direction which constitutes the good life is that which is selected by the total organism, when there is psychological freedom to move in **any** direction" (pp. 186–187).

The characteristics of the process include:

1. **Increasing openness to experience.** Threatening experiences are not denied nor distorted. The person, far from being defensive, is determined to "own" a wide variety of experiences that life presents. The person does not need to employ the mechanism of subception but enjoys full awareness of him or herself and of the environment.

2. **Increasing existential living.** Rogers (1961) explained existential living as follows: "The self and personality emerge **from** experience, rather than experience being translated or twisted to fit preconceived self-structure. It means that one becomes a participant in and an observer of the ongoing process of organismic experience, rather than being in control of it" (pp. 188–189).

3. **Increasing trust in the organism.** Rather than looking for guidance to individuals or organizations, people use their own organism as their guiding force. The organism is not infallible, but the openness to experience helps correct errors quickly. For instance, anger is checked by the need for affiliation, affection, and relationship.

4. **Functioning more fully.** Drawing together the previous three points, Rogers (1961) characterized a fully functioning person as "more open to evidence from all sources, . . . soundly and realistically social; he lives more completely in this moment, but learns that this is the soundest living for all time" (pp. 191–192).

APPLICATIONS TO COUNSELING

Person-centered counselors are using Rogerian concepts as part of their theoretical orientation. Other helping professionals, however, may choose to incorporate at least some aspects of Rogers' theoretical framework:

1. His optimistic view of human nature—in proper perspective
2. The internal frame of reference focusing on the inner world of the client
3. The concept of an inborn actualizing tendency in every person
4. The concept of congruence between organismic experiences and the self
5. The importance of the self-concept for personality adjustment

CHAPTER REVIEW

1. What significant events from Rogers's life do you remember, and how may some of them have affected his theory?
2. What are the main points of emphasis in Rogers's theory?
3. What is meant by the internal frame of reference?
4. What does Rogers postulate as the basic human motivation?
5. How does Rogers define the organism and its functions?
6. How does Rogers view the self, particularly in its relationship with organismic experiences?
7. What is meant by congruence between organismic experiences and the self?
8. How does this congruence relate to a positive self-concept, and what implications can be drawn on psychological health?
9. How does the self-concept develop?
10. What is meant by the ideal self and the real self, and how is the difference between them measured?
11. What does Rogers mean by the "good life"?
12. Which aspects of Rogerian theory are applicable to the work of counseling practitioners?

REFERENCES

Rogers, C. R. (1959). A theory of therapy, personality, and interpersonal relationships, as developed in the client-centered framework. In S. Koch (Ed.). *Psychology: A study of a science* (Vol. 3, pp. 184–256). New York: McGraw-Hill.

Rogers, C. R. (1977). *Carl Rogers on personal power.* New York: Delacorte Press.

Rogers, C. R. (1951). *Client-centered therapy.* Boston: Houghton-Mifflin.

Rogers, C. R. (1983). *Freedom to learn for the 80's.* Columbus, OH: Merrill.

Rogers, C. R. (1961). *On becoming a person.* Boston: Houghton-Mifflin.

Smith, M. B. (1950). The phenomenological approach in personality theory: Some critical remarks. *Journal of Abnormal Psychology, 45,* 516–522.

CHAPTER 13

HOLISTIC THEORY

THE TERM "holism" has its origin in the Greek word "holos" that means complete or unified. When applied to the study of personality, the holistic approach emphasizes the psychosomatic unity and the uniqueness of every individual. The theory has much in common with phenomenology and self-theory covered in the two previous chapters. It also draws some of its concepts from Gestalt psychology and uses existentialism as its philosophical basis.

The two representatives of the holistic theory of personality presented in this chapter are Kurt Goldstein and Abraham Maslow. The difference between their approaches lies primarily in the sources from which they had drawn their data. Whereas Goldstein did most of his research on brain-injured soldiers, Maslow focused on the study of healthy persons.

KURT GOLDSTEIN (1878-1965)

Kurt Goldstein was born in a small town in Silesia, then part of Germany, now a province of Poland. After his elementary and secondary education (classical gymnasium with emphasis on the study of Greek and Latin literature and culture), he enrolled at the University of Breslau where he earned a doctorate in medicine. He became interested in neurology and psychiatry while doing research in Koenigsberg; his work earned him a professorship of neurology at the University of Frankfurt. It was during his tenure at Frankfurt that he conducted a major research study of brain-injured soldiers. In 1930, he was offered the directorship of the neurological unit of the well-known Moabit Hospital in Berlin.

When Hitler came to power, Goldstein was detained by the secret police and released only after he agreed to permanently leave Germany. He found a warm reception and a temporary home in the Netherlands, where he was offered a professorship at the University of Amsterdam. There he completed his major work, *The organism,* that contains the basic propositions of his personality theory.

Soon, however, Goldstein decided to emigrate to the United States. After arriving in 1935 in New York, he served as clinical professor of psychiatry at Columbia University and later at Tufts Medical School in Boston. Eventually, he went into private practice in neurology and psychiatry while maintaining professional contacts with several universities in the New York area.

In his later years Goldstein identified increasingly with phenomenology and existentialism in addition to Gestalt psychology, which was always prominent in his theoretical orientation. He died in New York City at the age of eighty-six.

POINTS OF EMPHASIS IN GOLDSTEIN'S THEORY

Four salient issues characterize Goldstein's theory:

1. **Holistic view of personality.** Goldstein viewed personality as a unified and fully integrated entity rather than a sum of components. He ascribed to personality a single motivational drive that helps promote its growth and maintain its constancy. In Goldstein's view, the terms **organism** and **personality** were interchangeable, but he used the term organism almost exclusively.

2. **Influence of Gestalt psychology.** Goldstein interpreted human behavior in gestaltist terms. The variety of behaviors a person typically employs during a single day should be understood as an ongoing sequence of dynamic processes in which one function emerges into figure while others fade into ground.

3. **The organism in social context.** Goldstein's theory perceived the organism in its logical relation to the environment. Goldstein thus blended his own brand of phenomenology with theoretical elements absorbed from Adler and several of his followers. This explains his strong emphasis on social elements for a healthy structure and development of personality.

4. **Concrete and abstract behavior.** Research on brain-damaged patients provided Goldstein with data for explaining healthy versus unhealthy operations of the organism. He dealt with this dichotomy on the basis of concrete and abstract operational patterns.

UNIFIED NATURE OF THE ORGANISM

In Goldstein's (1963) view, the organism is a unified Gestalt, not a mere accumulation of factors that are added to each other like bricks. Various conditions in which the organism finds itself stimulate a variety of actions or behaviors that seem to be directed toward unrelated goals. In reality, however, such actions prove that the organism possesses a broad repertoire of functions, which are mutually related (Goldstein, 1939).

This holistic functioning of the organism flows from the single motivational force of **self-actualization**: "The tendency to actualize itself is the motive which sets the organism going; it is the **drive** by which the organism is moved" (Goldstein, 1963, p. 140). Various drives that may be perceived as separate motivational forces, e.g., hunger, sexual urge, etc., are merely expressions of the same basic drive toward self-actualization. Instead of saying that a person is satisfying his or her hunger by having a meal, it is proper to call the individual's food intake self-actualization through eating.

Strictly speaking, "the concept of different separate drives is based on observations of the sick, of young children, and of animals under experimental conditions . . . in which some activities of the organism are isolated from the whole" (Goldstein, 1963, p. 142).

BEHAVIOR AS A FIGURE-GROUND INTERACTION

In an earlier discussion of Gestaltist influences on phenomenology, the figure-ground interaction was presented as an aid for explaining the process of human perception. In contrast to that view, Goldstein applies the figure-ground principle in a much broader perspective. He uses it not only to explain human perception, but also all other activities, in which one part of the organism acts on its own, distinct from the rest.

All behavior is interpreted in Goldstein's theory as a figure-ground interaction. For instance, when we speak, those organismic functions related to speech emerge as figure whereas the rest of the organism lapses into ground. The same happens when we raise our arm or make another gesture that adds emphasis to the spoken word. Goldstein (1963) believed, however, that figure and background are connected.

> The most superficial glance at the way we walk will show that the correct movements of our legs in walking depend upon definite movements of our

> arms and head. When for any reason freedom of arms and head is impeded, the gait changes immediately; in short, when the background changes, the figure (the performance) also changes. (p. 13.)

By this figure-ground interpretation of behavior, Goldstein emphasized the unity and integration of personality. Outside stimuli promote the formation of numerous figures in succession, which soon lapse into ground. This ongoing cycle of organismic differentiations repeats itself, again and again, throughout our waking hours.

To maintain a degree of equilibrium in the organism, Goldstein postulated the mechanism of **equalization.** This process helps the organism return to a state of relative balance after it has been incited to response in a particular way.

COMING TO TERMS WITH THE ENVIRONMENT

A healthy organism functions smoothly, with satisfaction to the individual, in a constant, well-ordered manner. The road toward self-actualization, however, is not without obstacles since the organism can assert itself "only in conflicting with and in struggling against, the opposing forces in the environment" (Goldstein, 1939, p. 305).

Needless to say, such environmental tensions produce a degree of anxiety in the individual. Unless such anxiety becomes debilitating, it should be tolerated as an inevitable condition of human existence. Eventually, however, every person has to **come to terms** with his or her environment.

The coming to terms can be achieved either by the willing acceptance of particular conditions in a given situation or, preferably, through an initiative of the organism that "overcomes the disturbance arising from the clash with the world, not out of anxiety but out of joy of conquest" (Goldstein, 1939, p. 305).

CONCRETE AND ABSTRACT BEHAVIOR

The research into the ability of the organism to engage in concrete or abstract behavior is mentioned here primarily because it is the hallmark of Goldstein's scientific accomplishments. He became involved in his research while treating brain-damaged soldiers in Germany.

Healthy persons with a well-functioning brain perform without difficulty both concrete and abstract tasks. Brain-damaged persons, however, are hindered in performing abstract operations.

Goldstein (1963) made a basic distinction between concrete and abstract behavior that can be stated, in simplified form, as follows: (1) concrete behavior is a **reaction** of the organism to "all that the individual perceives"; (2) abstract behavior is an **active** assessment of a situation; the individual has to "pick out the aspect which is essential, and act in a way appropriate to the whole situation" (pp. 59–60).

A case study presented by Goldstein clarifies this theoretical explanation: One of his patients was kind and affectionate to his family when on a home visit from the hospital (concrete situation). He seemed, however, totally disinterested in his wife and children after returning to the hospital since they were not physically present (abstract situation).

APPLICATIONS TO COUNSELING

Some concepts of Goldstein's theory may prove useful to present-day counselors, e.g.:

1. The concept of personality as an integrated organism
2. The striving of the organism for self-actualization, as the unifying motivational force
3. The challenge of coming to terms with the environment

ABRAHAM MASLOW (1908–1970)

Abraham Maslow was born in Brooklyn into a family of Jewish immigrants. The diaries he kept describe his unhappy youth and a family atmosphere full of tensions. There was an ongoing conflict between his strongly religious mother and his father, who was a vigorous man but who had a weakness for whiskey, women, and occasional disorderly conduct. Although successful in his school work, young Abe suffered from severe bouts of depression. At the age of eighteen he entered New York's City College, which provided for him a free undergraduate education.

A real boon to his mental health and personality growth came when he did graduate studies at the University of Wisconsin. Several professors gave special attention to this bright but naive young man and tried to make up for his underprivileged life in the East. Maslow studied under Professor Harlow and wrote his dissertation on the dominance in the behavior of monkeys. He stayed at Wisconsin for an additional year to do postdoctoral work.

The offer of a teaching position brought Maslow back to the East, where he taught for fourteen years at Brooklyn College. It was during this period in his life that he turned from behaviorism to a wider professional perspective and eventually to humanistic holism. During World War II Maslow began to explore human motivation in relation to lower and higher needs. He devoted time and energy to the study of the lives of self-actualizing individuals and to the role of values; he also became fascinated by a quasi-mystical phenomenon that he called "peak experiences."

From the early 1950s on, he held a position as professor of psychology at Brandeis University, where he remained for eighteen years. Toward the end of his career, he moved to California to accept a resident fellowship of the Laughlin Foundation in Menlo Park.

As his health was failing, he did some serious thinking about life and death. He would prefer to live a few years longer since he loved life, he was quoted as saying, but he did not really care that much (Massey, 1981). Maslow died in 1970 of a massive heart attack.

POINTS OF EMPHASIS IN MASLOW'S THEORY

Since the theories of Maslow and Goldstein have much in common, I will list here only a few points in which Maslow followed his own distinct course:

1. Although agreeing with Goldstein that the basic human motivation is manifested by the striving for self-actualization, Maslow accepted the existence of **specific needs** as motivational forces, which he placed in a hierarchy.

2. Whereas Goldstein made frequent references in his theory to the medical field, Maslow was closely attuned to philosophical, cultural, and religious concerns.

3. Goldstein considered the person's coming to terms with the environment to be an important **condition** for achieving self-actualization; in contrast, Maslow focused on the intrapersonal growth of the individual

and viewed genuine contacts with the environment to be the **outcome** of self-actualization.

THE STRUCTURE OF HUMAN NEEDS

Although he considered the individual to be an integrated whole, Maslow (1970) was not reluctant to recognize the existence of specific human needs that motivate the person's behavior. The structure of all motivational forces is perceived on a continuum that extends from the **need-level** to the **B-level** ("B" stands for "being" in its profound meaning, i.e., the existence of oneself integrated with the total cosmic reality).

At the need-level the individual is motivated to strive for **tension reduction.** The **lower needs** (physiological and safety) promote the physiological survival of the individual; the **higher needs** (love and esteem) foster psychological comfort and personality growth. The self-actualization need represents the **transition** from the higher need-level to the B-level. At the B-level Maslow (1962) postulated **metavalues** (also called **metaneeds**), which relate to the highest reaches of the human potential.

Self-actualization is a never-ending process that moves in a dynamic sequence upward through a continuum. The higher the individual progresses, the "more profound happiness, serenity, and richness of the inner life" he or she may achieve (Maslow, 1970, p. 99).

THE NEED LEVEL: A HIERARCHY

The hierarchy of needs implies that the lower needs have been adequately satisfied before higher needs emerge. The process is epigenetic in nature—known to us from Erickson's theory—in which one item builds upon another in time and space. In Erikson's theory, one developmental stage has to be successfully completed (and its virtue generated) before the next stage can be entered with any hope for success.

In Maslow's theory, the epigenetic principle finds a parallel application: unless the needs of a particular hierarchical step have been satisfied to an **adequate degree**, the next upward hierarchical step will not emerge. This does not mean, however, that the person's needs must be **totally fulfilled** at every hierarchical level. Maslow (1971) points out that a person's complaints (he calls them "grumbles") about insufficient need gratification may, in fact, indicate a desire to move on to the next hierarchical need level.

Figure 20 offers a graphic representation of the hierarchy of human needs postulated by Maslow (1970). In epigenetic sequence, they are as follows:

1. **Physiological needs.** These are the most basic needs, and they are present in every human being from the very beginning of life—the need for oxygen, nourishment, certain minerals, etc. When frustrated, these needs exert a powerful pressure on all functions of personality. When a person is hungry, "all capacities are put into the service of hunger satisfaction and the organization of these capacities is almost entirely determined by the one purpose of satisfying hunger" (p. 37). The tension has to be resolved and homeostasis restored.

2. **Safety needs.** Every individual requires security and freedom from fear, anxiety, and chaos. Safety also involves structure, order, established limits, and protection from harm. Although these needs are important throughout a person's life, they are particularly strong during infancy and childhood.

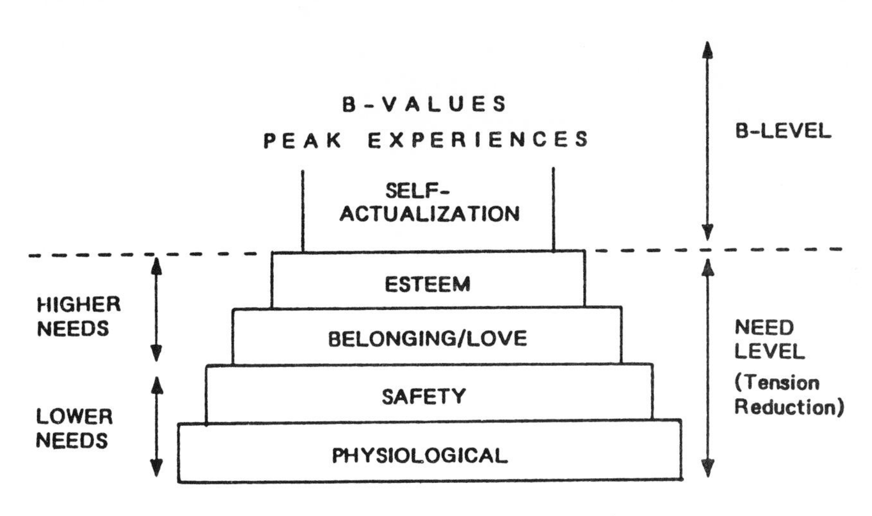

Figure 20. Diagram of Maslow's motivational structure.

3. **Belonging and love needs.** Once the lower needs are satisfied, the individual longs for love and affection and wants to belong. Being lonely, feeling ostracized, or having no roots are painful experiences. In Maslow's view, people living in a highly mobile society feel a great need for group membership. This is documented by the popularity of group counseling (T-groups and other growth groups).

4. **Esteem needs.** With the exception of certain pathological cases, all

people have these needs. Maslow (1970) subdivides these needs as they relate to the individual's strength and mastery (**self-esteem**) and as they relate to reputation, prestige, and recognition (**esteem of others**). He adds: "These needs have been relatively stressed by Alfred Adler and his followers, and have been relatively neglected by Freud" (p. 45).

5. **Need for self-actualization.** At this point, the individual moves up to the B-level—longing to become all he or she can be. Maslow (1970) stated emphatically: "What a man **can** be, he **must** be. He must be true to his own nature. . . . At this level, individual differences are greatest" (p. 46).

THE B-LEVEL: SELF-ACTUALIZATION AND BEYOND

Since the process of self-actualization is ongoing, a person is never fully self-actualized but continues striving. Maslow (1970) selected a sample of individuals whom he considered to be self-actualizing. Among them were both living persons whom he interviewed and historical figures whose lives and actions he analyzed. The group included Abraham Lincoln, Thomas Jefferson, William James, Aldous Huxley, Eleanor Roosevelt, and others.

Characteristics of Self-Actualizing Persons

Maslow (1970) identified fifteen characteristics that self-actualizing people have in common. Since many of the characteristics are similar to those ascribed by Combs and Snygg to adequate persons (see Chap. 11) and by Rogers to fully functioning persons (see Chap. 12), I will focus here only on the characteristics, which significantly add to the earlier-mentioned personality profiles:

Detachment and need for privacy. Self-actualizers can be alone without feeling lonely. Many of them positively cherish solitude and privacy.

Independence of culture and environment: autonomy and assertiveness. Self-actualizers depend more on their own judgment than on cultural norms and forge their life-styles in accordance with their own needs. They are self-disciplined, decisive, and responsible. Not depending on the approval of others, they possess "a relative stability in the face of hard knocks, blows, deprivations, frustrations, and the like" (Maslow, 1970, p. 162).

Sense of humor without hostility. The witticism of self-actualizers does not hurt others. It is directed at incongruencies inherent in a situation rather than at people's weaknesses.

Originality and creativity. Self-actualizers are imaginative people, and they use their imagination when dealing with various issues they encounter in their work, in their family life and child rearing, in art, etc.

Ego-transcendence: Maslow (1962) considered ego-transcendence to be the one **dominant** characteristic of every self-actualizing person:

> We are confronted with a difficult paradox when we attempt to describe the complex attitude toward the self or ego of the growth-oriented, self-actualized person. It is just this person, in whom ego-strength is at its height, who most easily forgets or transcends the ego, who can be most problem-centered, most self-forgetful, most spontaneous. (p. 34.)

Peak Experiences

The self-transcending attitude of an actualizing person is bound to B-cognition (cognition of being), which stands in contrast to the cognition of needs at the lower developmental stages. B-cognition is a unique concept of Maslow, saturated with existential overtones. B-cognition focuses on existence in its profound, universal meaning, and by its nature it leads to "peak experiences."

Such experiences are linked to moments of strong appreciation of beauty, goodness, or love. Maslow (1962) captured the impact of peak experiences in these words: "The emotional reaction in the peak experience has a special flavor of wonder, of awe, of reverence, of humility and surrender before the experience as before something great" (p. 82). The almost mystical sweep encountered here brings about an integration of the individual and the universe, and a trance-like oblivion of time and space.

B-Values

Individuals who experience reality in such profound dimensions find a fulfillment, which surpasses the pleasure of tension reduction at the need-level of their development. Although not all persons attain the B-level and participate in B-cognition, those who do, possess a system of values, which Maslow calls B-values. He lists among them: unity, destiny or fate, spontaneity, richness, simplicity, beauty or form, uniqueness, effortlessness, playfulness, honesty, and self-sufficiency.

These B-values are virtually identical with attitudes stimulated by peak experiences (Maslow, 1971), and they provide additional clues for identifying characteristics of self-actualizing people.

APPLICATIONS TO COUNSELING

Helping professionals who are involved in counseling or in organizational consultation may be able to use a number of concepts from Maslow's theory, particularly:

1. The concepts of needs and self-actualization
2. The concept of a need hierarchy and its implications on: (a) the psychological progress of clients, and (b) worker motivation and productivity
3. The concept of a self-actualized person and his or her characteristics
4. The concepts inherent in the B-level of human growth, i.e., peak experiences and B-values

CHAPTER REVIEW

1. Which events in Goldstein's life did you find of interest?
2. What does Goldstein mean by the unified nature of the organism and its basic motivational force?
3. How does Goldstein use gestaltist concepts to interpret human behavior?
4. What is meant by the need for the individual to come to terms with the environment?
5. How does Goldstein apply the study of concrete and abstract behavior to the assessment of brain functioning?
6. What do you consider interesting in Maslow's life?
7. How does Maslow's theory differ from Goldstein's?
8. What is meant by self-actualization?
9. What specific needs constitute Maslow's need hierarchy?
10. What are the characteristics of a self-actualizing person?
11. What is the meaning of the B-level of development, including peak experiences and B-values?
12. Which ideas of Goldstein or Maslow may be useful to present-day counselors?

REFERENCES

Goldstein, K. (1963). *Human nature in the light of psychopathology.* New York: Shocken.
Goldstein, K. (1939). *The organism.* New York: American Book Co.
Maslow, A. H. (1971). *The farther reaches of human nature.* New York: Viking.
Maslow, A. H. (1970). *Motivation and personality (2nd ed.).* New York: Harper & Row.
Maslow, A. H. (1962). *Toward a psychology of being.* New York: Van Nostrand.
Massey, R. F. (1981). *Personality theories: Comparisons and syntheses.* New York: Van Nostrand.

CHAPTER 14

LOGOTHERAPY

VIKTOR E. FRANKL (B. 1905)

THE ROOTS of Logotherapy are to be found in existentialism, phenomenology, and holism. Unlike many European existentialists, however, Frankl is neither pessimistic nor antireligious (Allport, 1962). In fact, his theory is a refutation of Nietzsche's nihilism that denied the existence of any meaning in human life. Frankl also opposed Freud's concept of will to pleasure and Adler's concept of will to power. Logotherapy, called "the third Viennese school of psychotherapy" (following Freud's and Adler's), is structured around its central concept of **will to meaning.**

Frankl's school is unique by the close linkage of its psychological theory and the underlying philosophical assumptions. The psychological and philosophical aspects of logotherapy are so closely interwoven that it is virtually impossible to separate them. Thus, logotherapy represents a personality theory holistic at its very core—totally integrated throughout its conceptual structure.

FRANKL'S LIFE

Viktor E. Frankl was born in 1905 into a Jewish family in Vienna. Even as a child, he was introspective and often surprised his elementary school teachers by the depth of his questions. An experience during his high school years had a profound influence on his thinking. When one of his fellow students was found, after committing suicide, with a book by Nietzsche at his side, Frankl became convinced of the strong power of philosophical ideas on a person's life and of the destructiveness of nihilism.

Still a youth, Frankl initiated contacts with Freud, who invited him to publish an article in the *International Journal of Psychoanalysis.* As a medical student, he became also a member of Adler's inner circle, but eventually grew disenchanted with the Adlerian movement. After graduation from medical school, Frankl embarked on a career in psychiatry. He is quoted as saying: "At that point, I suspended what I had learned from my great teachers and began listening to what my patients were telling me—trying to learn from them" (Fabry, 1968, p. 10).

In the 1930s, during the years of severe economic depression and unemployment, Frankl worked at the neuropsychiatric clinic of the University of Vienna. He spent much of his free time counseling distressed youth in advisory centers, which he founded. The rudiments of his theory were slowly emerging as he realized that many despondent youth who lost their jobs felt better when asked to do some work although without pay. For the unemployed young people the feeling of emptiness in life was far worse than the absence of a paying job.

When the German army occupied Austria, Frankl was given an opportunity to leave the country, but he decided to remain with his old parents. Eventually, he was summoned to report to Nazi authorities and was deported to a concentration camp. The inhuman treatment and personal degradation he experienced there proved to be the ultimate catalyst for his theory. Frankl's manuscript outlining the basic principles of logotherapy was destroyed by prison guards, but the ideas he had expressed lived on. In fact, the death camp experience refined his theory and gave it a new degree of strength and validity.

Shortly after his imprisonment, Frankl convinced himself and some of his fellow inmates that as long as they had something to live for, they would survive their imprisonment. Although reduced to a walking skeleton, he organized secret group discussions on mental health and gathered a circle of Alpine climbing devotees. Such sessions helped these despairing people look forward to engaging some day again in active work and in their favorite recreational activities.

After liberation, when Frankl returned to Vienna, he learned that his entire family, except for his sister, had been exterminated. In spite of this personal tragedy and the chaotic situation in the city, he resumed his professional work with great vigor and yet found sufficient time to earn a doctor's degree in philosophy, in addition to his medical degree. He wrote numerous books, many of them translated into foreign languages, and lectured extensively, both at the University of Vienna and throughout the world. He served as head of the Neurology Department at the Poliklinik Hospital of the city and was the founder of the Austrian

Medical Society of Psychotherapy. The government awarded him the Austrian State Prize for Public Education (Fabry, 1968).

Frankl has developed close ties with the United States, where he undertook about thirty lecture tours over the past decades. His American followers established the Institute of Logotherapy in Berkeley, California, which has its own publishing service.

MAIN EMPHASIS IN FRANKL'S THEORY

Frankl was concerned with the person as a whole, not merely with certain portions of personality. In his view, human nature is three-dimensional: It has (1) a physiological dimension, (2) a psychological dimension, and (3) a **noölogical** dimension. The third dimension is related to the individual's **will to meaning.** The central theme of Frankl's theory of personality focuses on the ongoing process of finding meaning in various situations of life.

The term **logotherapy** is derived from the Greek noun "logos," which means word or meaning. Meaning of life contains a spiritual dimension. Frankl cautioned, however, that the term **spiritual** is not necessarily linked with religion, particularly not with a religious creed. It is up to individuals to decide **whether** or **to what degree** they will add religious connotations to the meaning of their lives.

FREEDOM OF WILL

As an existentialist, Frankl (1978) postulated the freedom of will as a basic human attribute, although at times the exercise of freedom may require a major effort: "Human freedom is a finite freedom. Man is not free from conditions. But he is free to take a stand in regard to them. The conditions do not completely condition him. Within limits it is up to him whether or not he succumbs and surrenders to the conditions. He may as well rise above them" (p. 47).

Frankl (1965) believed that the individual's freedom was also limited by intrapersonal factors, which he called **destiny.** As a phenomenologist, he emphasized the importance of our present perceptions, but he was equally aware of the influence of past events on our choices. Because of this awareness, he postulated his concept of destiny: "We must never forget that all human freedom is contingent upon destiny to the extent that it can unfold only within destiny and by working upon it" (p. 78).

However, contrary to Freud's opinion that high levels of hunger would produce identical expressions of the one unsatisfied urge, Frankl (1978) argued that in the concentration camp hunger made some people into beasts and others into saints. Instead of accepting physiological determinism, he repeated Magda Arnold's statement, "All choices are caused but they are caused by the chooser" (p. 48).

WILL TO MEANING

As was earlier mentioned, Frankl postulated three dimensions of personality—physiological, psychological, and noölogical (or noetic). Neglect of physiological needs leads to physical illness and neglect of psychological needs is the cause of emotional problems. Since the noölogical dimension is as important as the other two, neglecting its needs causes problems at the very core of personality. To satisfy the basic noetic needs, the individual has to assert his or her **will to meaning.** Frankl (1978) agreed with Maslow that the will to meaning was "man's primary concern."

The will to meaning is closely linked with human freedom. Frankl made it quite clear that there is no parallel between the operation of basic instincts at the physiological level and the will to meaning at the noetic level. Basic drives are inborn, but "man is never driven to moral behavior; in each instance, he decides to behave morally. Man does not do so in order to satisfy a moral drive" (Frankl, 1962, p. 101).

A genuine will to meaning has to be the outcome of free decisions made by individuals on their own. Frankl (1978) added in a critical vein:

> It is precisely this will to meaning that remains unfulfilled by today's society—and disregarded by today's psychology. Current motivation theories see man as a being who is either **reacting** to stimuli or **abreacting** his impulses. They do not consider that actually, rather than reacting or abreacting, man is **responding**—responding to questions that life is asking him, and in that way fulfilling the meanings that life is offering. (p. 29.)

Frankl pointed out that his view on the will to meaning was supported by empirical evidence. He quoted, among others, two studies conducted in the United States by Johns Hopkins University on college students and by the University of Michigan on working people. The results of these studies indicated that people prefer to have a meaningful job over a well-paying job.

MEANING OF LIFE

As is typical of his approach, Frankl (1978) introduced this central concept of his theory by relating a personal experience. When he was thirteen years old, his science instructor commented during one of his classes that "life was nothing but a combustion process, an oxidation process." Without asking for permission to speak, Frankl jumped up and "threw him the question, 'What meaning, then, does life have?' " (p. 37). There was no response.

To search for the meaning of life is a major responsibility of every individual. Meaning cannot be artificially projected upon a situation. It is present in every situation the individual encounters, and is to be drawn from that situation. The meaning of life is not abstract but is as **concrete** and unique as the situation itself (Frankl, 1978). The individual needs to be open to situations he or she encounters and detect (differentiate) the meaning, which reflects each situation and his or her involvement in it:

> If the meaning which is waiting to be fulfilled by man were really nothing but a mere expression of self, or no more than a projection of his wishful thinking, it would immediately lose its demanding and challenging character; it could no longer call man forth or summon him.... I think the meaning of our existence is not invented by ourselves, but rather detected. (Frankl, 1962, pp. 100–101).

Every situation has its meaning contained within. Since the sequence of situations evolves from day to day and from hour to hour, the meanings of the current moment "are ever changing. But they are never missing" (Frankl, 1978, p. 39). Discovering these ever changing meanings throughout one's life is an ongoing challenge that every person faces:

> What man actually needs is not a tensionless state but rather the striving and struggling for some goal worthy of him. What he needs is not the discharge of tension at any cost, but the call of a potential meaning waiting to be fulfilled by him. What man needs is not homeostasis but what I call "noö-dynamics," i.e., the spiritual dynamics in a polar field of tension where one pole is represented by a meaning to be fulfilled and the other pole by the man who must fulfill it. (Frankl, 1962, p. 107).

Frankl (1962) pointed out that the individual can discover "meaning in life in three different ways: (1) by doing a deed, (2) by experiencing a value, (3) by suffering" (p. 113). These three ways of discovering meaning in life need to be further explored.

Doing a Deed

Anything we do—our job, our hobby, sports activities, etc.—falls into the category of doing a deed. Frankl argues that every activity contains a hidden meaning. A carpenter can find meaning in his or her work by looking at the quality of the product and the honest effort he or she puts into the project. A housekeeper in a motel can find meaning in the cleanliness and orderliness of the room she or he has prepared for the next guest.

On the other hand, work involvement (a deed), which by its very nature is uplifting and valuable, can be rendered meaningless, if it is done in a self-centered way, without consideration of others. For instance, an artist who is painting strictly with the profit purpose in mind, will produce "trendy" paintings that follow current fads, but will give little or no thought to the dimensions of beauty, artistic honesty, and good taste of his or her work. Even helping professionals can, because of self-centeredness or lack of care, seriously compromise the obligations they have assumed, render their work meaningless, and at times, endanger their clients or patients.

To turn a routine activity into a meaningful human deed, one has to direct it beyond oneself. For instance, "a dialogue that is restricted to mere self-expression does not participate in the self-transcendent quality of the human reality" (Frankl, 1978, p. 66). **Self-transcendence** does not necessarily involve heroic actions. Any seemingly insignificant act that is done with consideration of others becomes self-transcendent, truly human, and meaningful.

Experiencing a Value

By experiencing a value Frankl meant any **genuine** human experience that is **enriching** or uplifting. This may be exposure to good art, to the beauty of nature, or to humane accomplishments. Frankl (1965) considered love to be the highest value-related human experience: "Love enormously increases receptivity to the fullness of values. The gates to the whole universe of values are, as it were, thrown open" (p. 133). It may be a relationship that exists between lovers genuinely committed to each other; it may be the closeness that has persisted over the years between old friends; it may be the love parents feel for their children (**filia**), or the spiritualized love of a person who is dedicated to the service of others (**agape**). In Frankl's view, only through love do we become fully aware of another person's inner self.

Human love can thus be understood as a **caring** attitude, e.g., professional dedication in the service of society. This is identical with the individual's long-term meaning in life, which Frankl (1962) called a vocation:

> Everyone has his own specific vocation or mission in life to carry out a concrete assignment which demands fulfillment. Therein he cannot be replaced, nor can his life be repeated. Thus, everyone's task is as unique as is his specific opportunity to implement it. (pp. 110–111.)

All short-term, transient and momentary, meanings that the individual has discovered from early youth on should lead to a **long-term meaning** of life, i.e., to a personal vocation. A diagram of this interaction between short-term meanings and long-term vocation can be found in Figure 21.

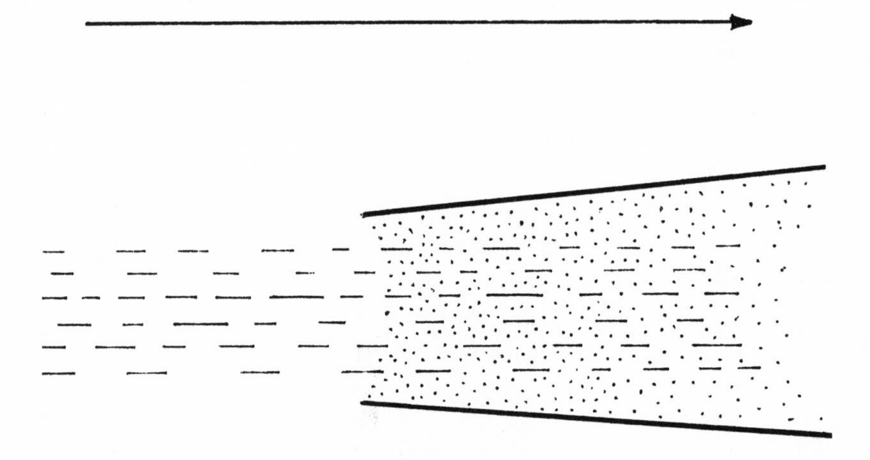

Figure 21. Short-term meanings related to individual deeds (short narrow lines) lead to the formation of a long-term vocation (dotted area between the two heavy lines). The arrow on top indicates the direction of the developmental sequence.

For instance, a college student does honest work to complete a required course (doing a deed). This is repeated many times throughout the years of study. As a result, the student will graduate and enter a profession in which he or she can find a long-term meaning of life by performing the job-related duties with utmost care for others and with genuine personal satisfaction.

Suffering

Although suffering should never be sought, it is nevertheless present in every human life. In Frankl's (1965) view, "human life can be fulfilled not only in creating and enjoying, but also in suffering. . . . Great artists, in particular, have understood and described this phenomenon of inner fulfillment in spite of outward failure" (p. 106).

Logotherapy refers to the **tragic triad**—suffering, guilt, and death—as providing opportunities for the most profound human growth: "Whenever one is confronted with an inescapable, unavoidable situation, whenever one has to face a fate which cannot be changed, . . . one is given a last chance to actualize the highest value, to fulfill the deepest meaning, the meaning of suffering. For what matters above all is the attitude we take toward suffering" (Frankl, 1962, p. 114).

Frankl (1965) pointed out that unlike psychoanalysis, which makes patients capable of coping with relatively pleasant life situations, logotherapy helps them develop attitudes for coping with suffering. The sufferer becomes a hero who turns suffering into **moral achievement** and thus discovers life's ultimate meaning. A clinical case study of Frankl relates the statement of a slowly dying man that seems to parallel Maslow's peak experiences: "I was filled with emotion of love for all mankind, a sense of cosmic vastness" (p. 115).

Frankl decries the unwillingness of modern society to come to terms with suffering and quotes Edith Weisskopf-Joelson to prove his point. This American psychologist points out "unhealthy trends in the present-day culture of the United States, where the incurable sufferer is given very little opportunity to be proud of his suffering and to consider it ennobling rather than degrading" so that "he is not only unhappy, but also ashamed of being unhappy" (Frankl, 1962, p. 116).

EXISTENTIAL VACUUM

People whose lives are devoid of meaning suffer from what logotherapy terms "existential vacuum." According to Frankl (1978), existential vacuum is at the root of a great number of suicides, particularly among apparently successful and affluent people. A study of attempted suicides among college students revealed that the feeling of **meaninglessness** was the cause of suicidal behavior of 85 percent of the students: "Most important, however, 93 percent of these students suffering from the apparent meaninglessness of life 'were actively engaged socially, were performing well academically, and were on good terms with their family groups' " (p. 20).

Closely related to the phenomenon of existential vacuum is **Sunday neurosis.** In Frankl's view, the routine of their jobs makes people forget their inner emptiness while at work. During leisure hours, however, and particularly on weekends, the impact of the existential vacuum strikes them with full force, since they have time to reflect on their lives.

Frankl (1962) believes that "such widespread phenomena as alcoholism and juvenile delinquency would not be understandable unless we recognize the existential vacuum underlying them. This is also true of the crises of pensioners and aging people" (p. 109).

APPLICATIONS TO COUNSELING

Frankl's theory provides several concepts that may be applied to working with clients who seem bored with life or who are experiencing trauma. Counselors may find the theory useful even in their own lives. Of particular value may be the following concepts:

1. Freedom of will and will to meaning
2. The three ways of discovering meaning
3. Attitudes that help people cope with suffering
4. The concepts of existential vacuum and Sunday neurosis

CHAPTER REVIEW

1. Which personal experiences of Frankl influenced and additionally validated the theory of logotherapy?
2. What is the main emphasis in Frankl's theory?
3. Which philosophical and psychological movements have influenced Frankl's theory?
4. How did Frankl interpret the freedom of will?
5. Which three dimensions did Frankl postulate in personality?
6. How did Frankl explain the meaning of life?
7. What are the three ways of discovering meaning of life?

8. How do the short-term meanings in one's life relate to and influence his or her long-term vocation?
9. What is meant by the tragic triad?
10. What is meant by the **ultimate** meaning in life?
11. How does Frankl explain the concepts of existential vacuum and of Sunday neurosis?
12. How could some of Frankl's concepts enrich the lives of counselors and add effectiveness to their work?

REFERENCES

Allport, G. W. (1962). Preface. In V. E. Frankl. *Man's search for meaning* (pp. ix–xii). New York: Simon & Schuster.

Fabry, J. B. (1968). *The pursuit of meaning: Logotherapy applied to life.* Boston: Beacon Press.

Frankl, V. E. (1965). *The doctor and the soul: From psychotherapy to logotherapy.* New York: Knopf.

Frankl, V. E. (1962). *Man's search for meaning.* New York: Simon & Schuster.

Frankl, V. E. (1978). *The unheard cry for meaning: Psychotherapy and humanism.* New York: Simon & Schuster.

CHAPTER 15

PERSONALITY THEORIES IN PERSPECTIVE

NO MATTER for what purpose you read this book, it likely solidified two conclusions you may have formed earlier: (1) Human personality is a **complex**, fascinating phenomenon that retains elements of mystery in spite of concerted research. (2) The complex nature of personality is but one reason for the variety of theories covered in this book. Another reason lies in the **divergent** approaches used by the theorists.

From the field of personality theories, we covered about twenty of the more prominent ones—a fairly representative sample. Freud's psychoanalysis and Jung's analytic psychology emphasized the role of the **unconscious.** Others such as Adler, Horney, and Sullivan portrayed personality in the **social** context. We became aware of the strong disagreement that exists between self-theorists and behaviorists. Rogers, Maslow, and others representing the former school of thought emphasized the role of the **self** as catalyst of all personality dynamics and locus of human development. Hull and Skinner were among forceful spokespersons of behaviorism offering a technology that can effect changes of human **behavior** for more efficient coping with life. Finally, there were some theorists who promoted a **philosophical** approach to the study of personality, among them Fromm, Allport, and Frankl.

Because of the multiplicity of these theoretical orientations, this chapter presents a **classification** of the theories on a **continuum.** The continuum extends between two polarities based on philosophical assumptions about the **nature** of personality. While other taxonomies may be equally useful, the proposed classification system is preferable for the purpose of this book. It allows you, the reader, to clarify the position of individual theories, their similarities and contrasts, and—at least indirectly—your own theoretical leaning.

HOW TO FORM ONE'S OWN THEORY OF PERSONALITY

The Role of Life Experiences

As was mentioned in Chapter 1, virtually all major theories of personality are marked by salient life experiences of their originators. Freud's Oedipus conflict was related to the childhood experiences of Freud with his relatively old and stern father and a much younger, tender mother. The central concept of personal identity in Erikson's theory reflected young Erik's alienation from the Jewish community because of his Scandinavian origins and from the gentile environment because of his membership in the synagogue. Rogers's insistence on the need for individual freedom and his recommendation to listen to one's organism for clues in various life situations were undoubtedly reactions to his experiences in youth: a rigorous family upbringing, self-denial, and strict parental supervision. Another striking example is offered by Frankl's logotherapy, which was largely formulated in the brutal concentration camp atmosphere during World War II.

This close relationship of one's experiences and the way he or she interprets personality applies, of course, not only to theorists whose work has received wide acclaim, but to you, the reader, as well. On the basis of your knowledge of a broad spectrum of theories that you studied, you will be able to formulate your own theoretical framework to interpret personality dynamics.

Adopting an Established Personality Theory

Some students in the helping professions are attracted to a particular theory of personality, which seems to reflect their own values and with which they can readily identify. Since no one can relive the life of the theorists, however, even if you **adopt** a theory you will have to adjust it somewhat to your own personal situation. This may involve an increased emphasis of specific parts of the theory and deemphasis of others.

Adjustments are needed particularly for two reasons: (1) A theorist may have applied his or her theoretical concepts, which are challenging in themselves, too rigidly or too dogmatically. (2) Along with generally applicable ideas, a theory may contain other elements valid in their historical and cultural context but not applicable to our present conditions. This is the case when age ranges are suggested for developmental stages or when certain sociocultural phenomena, such as perceived male and female sex-roles, are discussed.

Structuring an Eclectic Framework

Some students make an effort to formulate an eclectic approach to personality during their professional preparation. Even those students, however, who at first adhere to only one theory will, during their professional career, broaden their perspective. Theoretically puristic attitudes, exclusively committed to a particular orientation, are rarely found in the real world of the helping professions.

There is certainly no ideal eclectic approach that will suit every person's interests and approximate his or her value structure. A logical, well-integrated brand of eclecticism stands, however, in marked contrast to an uncritical, haphazard accumulation of bits and pieces of various theories without any common denominator. To formulate a balanced, well-integrated eclectic interpretation of personality, two conditions should be met: (1) One should gain a solid knowledge of the major theories of personality; superficial knowledge is misleading. (2) One should develop a high degree of self-awareness in order to assess the relationship between the various theoretical concepts and his or her own life experiences and values.

The ultimate *raison d'etre* of personality theory is to facilitate the helping process. Since the personality of the helper is the **main tool** in the helping process, it follows that the helper's own self has to feel comfortable with the theoretical framework he or she uses for understanding the psychodynamic processes in clients.

CLASSIFICATION OF THEORIES

Two Polarities

In this classification system, two polarities serve as anchor points for a continuum. The two polarities were chosen on the basis of (1) contrasting definitions of personality and (2) contrasting frames of reference used for observing human behavior.

1. **Definitions of personality.** Polarity "A" is associated with theories that define personality as a mere **inference of behavior** (e.g., Cattell, 1950;

Dollard & Miller, 1950; Sullivan, 1953). In this view, personality is not real and has no functions of its own.

Polarity "B" is associated with theories that define personality as a real entity, possessing its own existence and functions (e.g., Allport, 1937, 1961; Combs & Snygg, 1959; Maslow, 1970).

2. **Frames of reference for observing behavior.** Combs and Snygg (1959) explain the contrast between the **objective** or **external** and the **perceptual** or **internal** frame of reference in these terms:

> Human behavior may be observed from at least two very broad frames of reference: from the point of view of an outsider, or from the point of view of the behaver himself. Looking at behavior in the first way we can observe the behavior of others and the situation in which such behavior occurs. . . . This is the "objective" or "external" frame of reference. The second approach seeks to understand behavior by making its observations from the point of view of the behaver himself. It attempts to understand the behavior of the individual in terms of how things "seem" to him. This frame of reference has been called the "perceptual" [or "internal"] . . . frame of reference. (p. 16.)

The external frame of reference is **objective;** it lends itself to **measurement** and to **evaluation** of behavior as normal or abnormal. Maturity is perceived in terms of **social adjustment,** which occurs through interaction with the environment. The individual's **freedom of choice** is **limited** by external or internal factors.

The perceptual or internal frame of reference is **subjective,** since it views behavior from the vantage point of the behaver by "walking in his or her moccasins." It does **not evaluate** behavior by comparing it with the typical behavior of the majority and does not label it "normal" or "abnormal." It perceives growth of the person in terms of **self-enhancement** and **personal adequacy,** which occur primarily from within. A major emphasis is placed on the individual's **freedom of choice.**

The Continuum

Between the two polarities extends the continuum on which we may visualize the relative positions of the theories covered in this book (see Fig. 22). If one of the polarities would be colored yellow and the other blue, the major part of the continuum would appear in various shades of green.

The position of each theory on the continuum should be considered a mere approximation of its actual location. Some theories should be

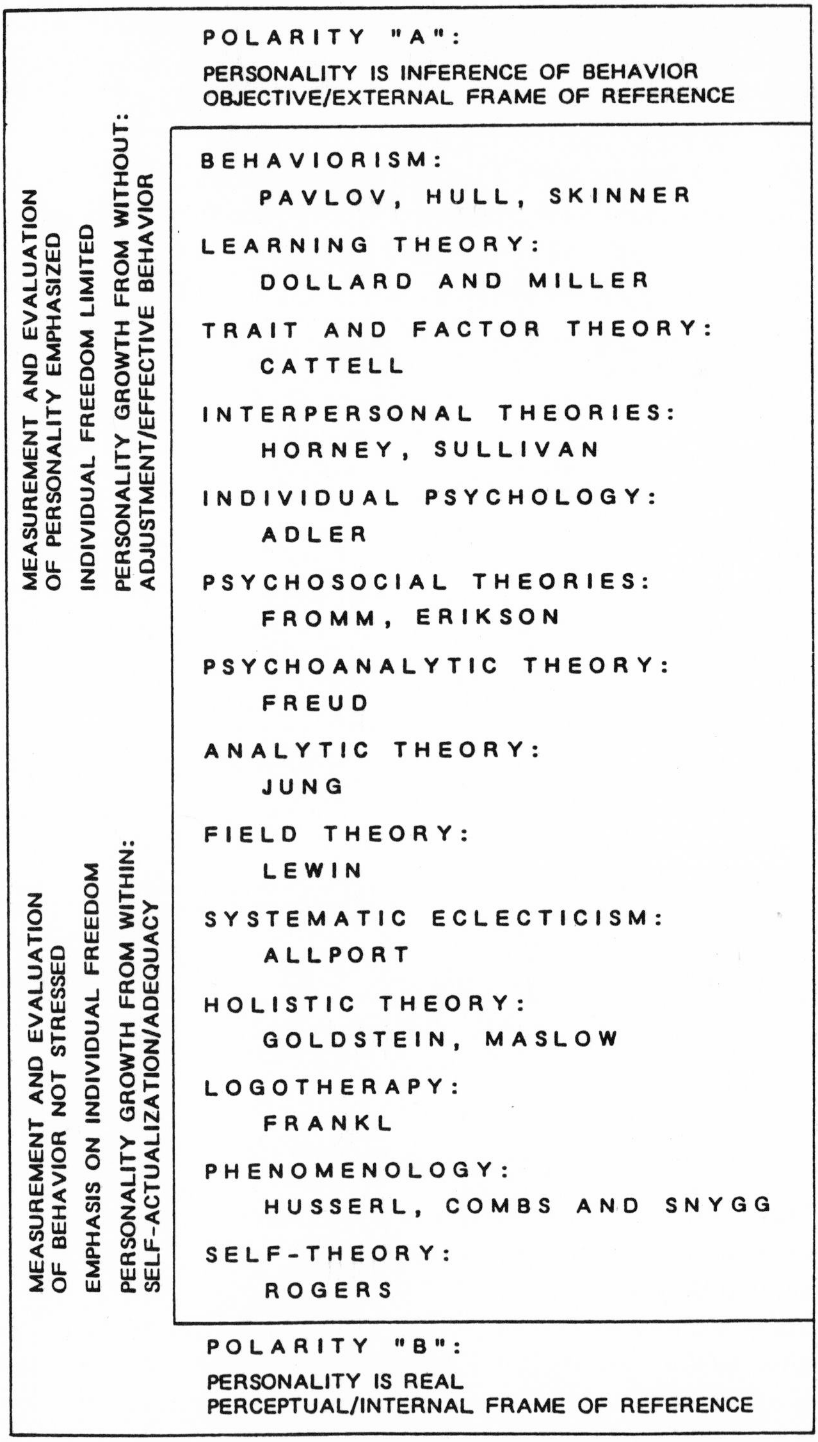

POLARITY "A":

PERSONALITY IS INFERENCE OF BEHAVIOR
OBJECTIVE/EXTERNAL FRAME OF REFERENCE

MEASUREMENT AND EVALUATION OF PERSONALITY EMPHASIZED

INDIVIDUAL FREEDOM LIMITED

PERSONALITY GROWTH FROM WITHOUT: ADJUSTMENT/EFFECTIVE BEHAVIOR

BEHAVIORISM:
PAVLOV, HULL, SKINNER

LEARNING THEORY:
DOLLARD AND MILLER

TRAIT AND FACTOR THEORY:
CATTELL

INTERPERSONAL THEORIES:
HORNEY, SULLIVAN

INDIVIDUAL PSYCHOLOGY:
ADLER

PSYCHOSOCIAL THEORIES:
FROMM, ERIKSON

PSYCHOANALYTIC THEORY:
FREUD

ANALYTIC THEORY:
JUNG

FIELD THEORY:
LEWIN

SYSTEMATIC ECLECTICISM:
ALLPORT

HOLISTIC THEORY:
GOLDSTEIN, MASLOW

LOGOTHERAPY:
FRANKL

PHENOMENOLOGY:
HUSSERL, COMBS AND SNYGG

SELF-THEORY:
ROGERS

MEASUREMENT AND EVALUATION OF BEHAVIOR NOT STRESSED

EMPHASIS ON INDIVIDUAL FREEDOM

PERSONALITY GROWTH FROM WITHIN: SELF-ACTUALIZATION/ADEQUACY

POLARITY "B":

PERSONALITY IS REAL
PERCEPTUAL/INTERNAL FRAME OF REFERENCE

Figure 22. Classification of personality theories covered in this book.

closer together, while others should be farther apart. For instance, there should be a greater distance between Cattell's trait and factor theory and the interpersonal theories represented by Horney and Sullivan.

We also need to recognize that there are few "purebred" theories. This is particularly true of theories in the central section of the continuum, but it applies also to some theories close to either end. An example is Goldstein's holistic theory. Its emphasis on gestaltist, phenomenological, and existential ideas draws it very close to polarity "B." But its stress on coming to terms with the environment reflects the social dimension of personality growth and would move it closer to the center of the continuum.

A POSTSCRIPT

As we traversed the field of personality theories, we have gained many insights. We learned about the dynamics of people's motivation and internal growth and observed their inner conflicts, anxieties, and failures. Acquiring this new perspective on life is enriching in itself. It may have shed light on our own behavior and clarified the reasons why some people around us act the way they do.

The more we have learned, however, the more we should realize that this is just a beginning. To unlock the door that leads to the knowledge of the person is a never-ending challenge. As long as we live, we will find new and surprising facets of personality that have escaped us at earlier times.

It is a universally recognized axiom that knowledge is power. For helping professionals, a solid knowledge of personality theories augments their power of professional competence. It may also strengthen their caring attitudes since understanding fosters empathy.

CHAPTER REVIEW

1. Which conclusions did the reading of this book solidify for you?
2. What are some of the divergent approaches of personality theorists that you became aware of?
3. Can you offer examples of experiences in the lives of theorists that influenced the nature of their theories?
4. Which of your own experiences and values may have a bearing on forming your own personality theory?

5. Which two ways of forming your own theory are available to you?
6. Which conditions have to be fulfilled for the formation of a balanced eclectic theory?
7. What is the structure of the classification system used for personality theories in this book?
8. On what basis were the two polarities (anchor points for the continuum) chosen?
9. How should you perceive the position of individual theories on the continuum?
10. In what way does the study of personality have a bearing on our personal and professional life?

REFERENCES

Allport, G. W. (1961). *Patterns and growth in personality.* New York: Holt, Rinehart & Winston.

Allport, G. W. (1937). *Personality: A psychological interpretation.* New York: Holt, Rinehart & Winston.

Cattell, R. B. (1950). *Personality: A systematic and factual study.* New York: McGraw-Hill.

Combs, A. W., & Snygg, D. (1959). *Individual behavior: A perceptual approach to behavior.* New York: Harper & Row.

Dollard, J., & Miller, N. E. (1950). *Personality and psychotherapy: An analysis in terms of learning, thinking, and culture.* New York: McGraw-Hill.

Maslow, A. H. (1970). *Motivation and personality* (2nd ed.). New York: Harper & Row.

Sullivan, H. S. (1953). *The interpersonal theory of psychiatry.* New York: Norton.

INDEX